The Bible For Black Girls

a collection of texts posts from tumblr user pinkvelourtracksuit

written by: **Chelsea Claverie**

organized by: **DeKeshia S. Horne**

CONTENTS

*

DEDICATION

From Chelsea aka Tumblr user pinkvelourtracksuit (previously known as pink-vulva): This book is dedicated to all the black girls and anyone who follows me. I love ya'll and the support means so much to me.

i am here for ALL black women. i am here for my black trans women! i am here for black girls that rock weaves! i am here for baby girl that's rocking the afro puffs! i am here for the black girls with slender petite frames! i am here for my plus sized black women! i am here for black women of all shapes and sizes! i am here for my black girls that have short hair! i am here for my black girls with long hair! i am here for black girls that are unsure of themselves! i am here for black girls that are confident as fuck! i am here for dark skin girls! i am here for light skin girls! i am here for black girls that are every shade in between! i am here for ALL black girls!!!!!!! i love all of ya'll. ya'll are so cute! and i'm proud of ya'll. i'm proud of us. we're sisters! we're going to continue to slay and challenge Eurocentric beauty standards together and just generally go awfff!!!!

From DeKeshia: Thank you Chelsea for allowing me to put this together and I hope you enjoy this as well as many others have come to enjoy your blog.

NOTES

This book is a collection of Chelsea's (aka pinkvelourtracksuit from blogging site Tumblr) text posts from roughly 2011-2014. I was given her permission to organize them into a book for herself and the people that follow her blog. Her italicized text quickly became popular because of its inspiring and relatable content. I did my best to categorize them so that they could be easier to read. Hope you enjoy. All illustrations and artwork done by Chelsea Claverie.

NOTE TO SELF (& YOU TOO)

NOTE TO SELF: UR BEAUTIFUL, SMART, AND INCREDIBLE! AND U
WILL GO SO FAR! DON'T LET THE DEVIL TELL U THAT U DON'T
DESERVE GOOD THINGS! HE'S A LIAR AND A HATER!!!!!!

*

*just a reminder! don't forget to thank God for ur ass and titties today! be
grateful!!!!!*

*note to self: don't fall victim to seeking a nigga's approval and letting a nigga give
you self esteem issues and never compare yourself to other bitches.*

*when ur having a rough day
just think back to how u looked in 2009 <3*

IDK BOUT U BUT ima stan for myself and God.

*note to self: stop worrying about niggas and focus on graduating school baby
girl !!!!!! because niggas will come and go honestly! Think of that money u gone get
when u get that high salary paying job. fuck these niggas. don't u dare skip class
to hang out with none of these bum ass niggas. study for that test u got coming up
instead of talking to that nigga on the phone. get it together!!!!!!*

i'm too good for 100% of the niggas i come across.

*note to self: ur beautiful. ur skin will clear up and ur still beautiful even if
it doesn't.*

a lot of niggas are sleepin' on how great i am.

**clears throat*
repeat afta me
I LOOK
TOO GOOD
TO BE DEALING
WITH*

8

ANYBODY'S BULLSHIT.

one of the main things i'm learning to work on within myself is being envious or jealous of others who are in the place i want to be. like my friends are in healthy relationships and one of my homegirls is getting married and i crave that companionship low-key. I used to be angry and not understand why i don't have a nigga. i used to be scared (and i'm still a lil scared) that no one would ever be interested in me like that or whatever. that niggas will only see me as a piece of ass and not for the amazing person i am, but now i'm just chilling. It's not my time yet. I gotta be patient and positive. i'm just working on self improving and becoming a better me so when the time comes, i'll be ready :)

in private, i literally rip myself apart and destroy myself for not being perfect. i'm not perfect and it eats me up like a lot and it fucks with me. i compare myself to others a lot and that shit is so unhealthy for my well being. i love myself but i hate the way that i'm so unkind and mean to myself. i blame myself for not being perfect but being perfect is a fucking illusion. an unattainable unrealistic ass standard. that's what's so fucking crazy and insane about what i'm doing. i'm chasing something that's not even fucking real. i'm beating myself the fuck up and it's so exhausting and it's taking its toll on me mentally. i'm so tired man. i'm striving to be kind to myself. i want to just comfort myself and treat myself like a good friend. i'm 10 times harsher on myself than anyone else. i need to spend less time on the internet and more time out in the sun. i need to stop worrying about what the next bitch is doing and just focus on M E. me me me me me me me me me.

note to self: never be pressed over a nigga that isn't urs. if he ain't tryna claim u, he's just not that into u ma. keep ya options open. don't wait for no nigga. a real nigga that knows how beautiful, fly, and special u are will come into ur life and appreciate u.

next time u look in the mirror, take off all ur clothes ana literally spit game and holler at urself. it works i swea. just be like 'DAMNNNNNN SHITTT OOOOOOOO BITCH WUSSUP MA!' 'U LOOKIN GEWD!!!' 'U GOT A MAN BY ANY CHANCE?' 'BITCH LOOK AT CHUUU!!!! UR SICKENING!'

note to self: baby girl stop looking at his instagram. it ain't gone do nothing but disappoint ya ma.

God is honestly so real. i'm looking betta than all the people that teased me in high school, my ex, and his girl and i'm not even in my final form yet? like please!!!!!

comparing myself to others is honestly the most unhealthiest habit i have.

note to self: please be careful about the things u say or the thoughts u have because u can literally speak or think things into existence. only keep positive thoughts, don't let the negative thoughts creep up on u shawty! ur beautiful and ur special and u do have a purpose in this life! <3

2014 is not even over yet and i'm so proud of the woman i am rn. like bye.

note to self: don't let these niggas distract u from ya goals.

squeeze ya titties and grip ya booty meat to reduce stress.

note to self: u a bad lil bitch and u need to stop going out of ur way to please people who wouldn't piss on u if yo ass was on fire. Deal with people who are dependable. stop fucking with lame ass muthafuckas who don't keep their word. Do better ma, i know u can.

stan for no one but ya self and God. all ya favs will betray u and disappoint u in the end.

Dear God, it me. please protect me from the hoes that would love to see me fall off.

Dear God, it me again. please keep my skin clear, my ass fat, my eyebrows on fleek, and my titties sittin up right. amen.

note to self: stop dealing wit niggas who don't do shit for u. stop dealing with 'let's chill at the crib' niggas. at least make that nigga take u out to eat and court u. u deserve it. ur too cute to be dealing with niggas who only want pussy from u but won't even take u out to dinner or buy u something! and most importantly…don't ever fuck for free.

WANT a nigga but don't NEED a nigga.

quick lil reminder! just because a nigga buys u something or takes u out to eat doesn't mean u owe him shit!

note to self: get out of ur comfort zone so u can level the fuck up hoe! don't become complacent. u can always do better.

note to self: place ur emotional well being above everything else. if u don't want to take that class anymore, drop it. if u dealing with someone toxic whether it is a family member or a close friend, cut things off. if u want to cry, yell, and scream, do that. pay close attention to what triggers feelings of stress and sadness within u. protect ur emotional well being at all costs.

i still love being black regardless of the bullshit we go thru!

if u wanna do some amazing shit, get out of ur comfort zone.

man i gotta stop being bashful about looking at myself/fixing my hair in the mirror of a public bathroom. like so the fuck what if people think i'm vain or into myself. i am.

um i need to let go of the concept of 'getting my shit together' or whatever because my definition of 'getting my shit together' means perfection and i'll never be perfect but i'm damn near close to it so ima just have to accept that and ride out.org

I NEED TO STOP COMPARING MYSELF TO OTHER BITCHES.

don't look at his instagram. do. not. look. at. his. instagram.

when i'm having a rough day i just think about the positives. like the fact that i still look 18 yrs old, i'm young, black, and beautiful then i smile and realize my day isn't so bad after all.

i need to start taking better care of my body. i can't say that i love myself fully while eating junk and bullshit every day. i need to drink more water, eat more shit w/ nutritional value and be more active. it's not even about vanity anymore. sure, i want my body to be the truth but i'm just more worried about my health than anything at this point.

love urself
sleep w/ a satin pillowcase or scarf at nite
lay those edges before leaving the house
lotion ur elbows
take a bottle of h20 out w/ u to stay hydrated thru out the day
get a full night's rest
monitor how frequently u take a shit to insure that ur body is free of toxins
do this 4 urself ma.

clear ur mind. drink a glass of waturrrr. disinfect ur phone. disinfect ur laptop. wash ur bed sheets. listen to a lil andre 3000. light some incense. look at ur body from all angles in the mirror. learn every curve and couture of ur body. make a lil list of thangs to be grateful for.

why will i neva be good enough?....GOTCHAAAAA! i'm da baddest bitch!!!!!!!!!!! BYEEEEEE!!!!

note to self: big up urself! don't depend on any nigga to validate ur beauty. even on those days when u don't feel ur very best, know that ur still beautiful regardless! take more photos ma! from new angles! take care of ur body! it's the only one u'll ever have. eat more fruits and veggies. drink 2 liters of water everyday. Never let a nigga put any doubt in ur head that u are average because u are not. u are truly one of a kind.

i've been doing a lot of thinking and life is truly like a vehicle. i have control of the wheel and i can do simple small things that will either turn me in the right direction or turn me in the wrong direction. this sounds corny as hell but fuck it....i can have anything i want if i'm willing to do the work it takes to get it. the world is at my fingertips man. Nothing is out of my reach. if i want great things for my life, i have to stop being so comfortable and do shit that makes me uncomfortable and shit that i'm afraid of. i have to be brave and take chances because i only got one time to do this thang. i want a family and i want love so bad. all those nights i've cried in the shower. all those times i stayed awake thinking about that shit crying my eyes out because i'm so afraid of being alone yet i'm so terrified of being so close and so vulnerable with someone at the same time. wanting to have a career i love and being in love with someone that i can trust are things that i want so badly. right now, i'm just trying so hard to give myself everything that i need. i'm feeding my body with fruits,vegetables, and whole grains. i'm giving it water when it's thirsty. i sweat. i take warm showers. i walk around the house naked. i touch my body and i stare at it in the mirror a lot. i reflect on how i can improve and become a better person. i'm always thinking of ways i can make changes so that i can love myself because this year has really taught me that i have no one else in this world but me. i don't have my shit together but i'm slowly getting it together and it feels nice. I have to get this instant concept out of my head man. i be wanting everything NOW NOW NOW and i annoy the hell out of myself because i be expecting wild crazy shit NOW when i haven't done anything to get to that point in my life. I gotta chill out and just take shit one day at a time man. life really is about the simple things. Small actions add up to Big actions. big thangs. big shit. it's all about staying consistent with those small actions u feel me??

God didn't have to make me black and beautiful but he did and i just wanna take this time to thank him for that!!!!!

wifes myself up
gasses myself up
rubs my own titties
smacks my own ass
fucks myself

if it doesn't feel uncomfortable, u ain't growing or progressing.

what's hot in the streets rn
me

looks in the mirror
WHO DOES THIS FINE ASS BITCH THINK SHE IS?
squares up
IMA FIGHT THIS HOE FOR THINKING SHE LOOK GOOD.

i really gotta stay prayed up 24/7 because the devil be tryna murk a nigga.

note to self: never give all of urself to a nigga because niggas are temporary. they are disposable and can easily be replaced. these niggas will run u crazy ana have u thinking that something is wrong with u but meanwhile they be the problem.

looks in the mirror
BISHHHH LOOK ATCHUUU.
LOOK AT THAT ASS!
LOOK AT THEM TITTIES!
LOOK AT THAT FACE!
U NOTHIN BUT THE TRUTH MA!

it's 2k14! pls stop settling for mediocre ppl and things!

note to self: keep going baby girl, ur doing so well. ur gonna get ur shit together i promise just keep going. don't give up ma, u almost there!

i love looking in the mirror and looking even better than i expected!!!!! it's like GOTCHA BITCH! U LOOK GREAT. SHARE IT WIT THE WORLD GIRL.

things i need to stop doing
1. eating fast food
2. eating in my car
3. comparing myself to others
4. procrastinating
5. allowing myself to think negative thoughts

i really need to work on fully expressing how i feel in words and not just in writing. like if i'm angry or upset at someone, i sometimes feel ashamed or embarrassed to tell them?? i have to realize that my feelings are valid and they do matter so i can communicate them better.

i've been feeling so unmotivated and uninspired the past coupla months and I'm really just mentally trying to motivate myself and find things that i'm passionate about? because lately i've been on auto pilot and just nonchalant and numb about everything because it's much easier than feeling something? and i sometimes feel so trapped and helpless because time is moving by so fast and i want to make something out of myself before i get in that box in the ground and i'm so sick of not feeling anything about anything and i just want to feel some typa way about something and the fact that i don't is bothering me so much like? i hate school. i'm tired of studying for dumb ass classes that won't teach me anything important like how to be an actual adult and make adult decisions? and i'm tired of working a job that i don't love. also i'm tired of spending so much time on the computer/phone trying to escape my life? i can't live on auto pilot anymore. i really gotta start doing shit with my life. i don't want to be old as hell wishing i had done something with my youth. fuck that shit man.

from now on, ima keep people around me that's doing better than me not so i can hate on them and be envious on the sneak but just so i can be motivated and inspired to do better.

note to self: honestly no one can stop u from reaching ur full potential but u!!!!!!! u are ur own worst enemy!!! i'm proud of u for bouncing back and being able to redirect ur thoughts from negative to positive. ur going to do amazing things in 2015 baby!!!! i love u!

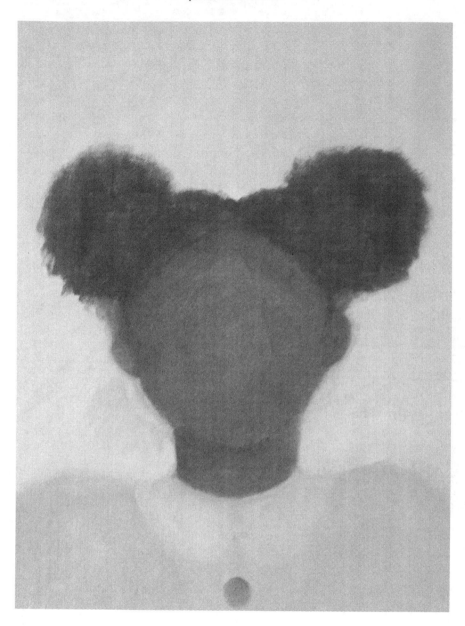

AESTHETIC

WEARS A JERSEY DRESS ON MY WEDDING DAY

*

let's tlk about the importance of baby hair and cheekbones.

current mood: ashanti's sideburns

shows up to ur funeral in a pink velour tracksuit, gold hoops, and corn rows

aaliyah + Kelis + Beyoncé = My Hair Idols

almost gets into a car crash because i can't stop looking at my eyebrows in the rear view mirror

when I'm home alone, I put on lotion and play music and pretend i'm in a world star candy video.

never leave the house without ur baby hair, ur cell phone, ur water bottle, and ur ankle bracelet.

i should have been in ginuwine's 'in those jeans' video rocking a pair of dark wash baby phat jeans topless back facing the camera with a tramp stamp tattoo showing, a rhinestone choker and sucking on a red lollipop but God petty.

i'm contemplating on whether I should wear the color black for the rest of my life.

I am 2003 Beyoncé, 2001 Jennifer Lopez, 2002 Ashanti, and 2004 Ciara rolled into one and you hoes are salty about it.

gotta smile that'll make yo nigga pre cum.

my aesthetic: 90's/early 2000's video vixen hoe.

sells my soul for a rare lisa frank notebook

u gotta show a lil nipple every now and again.

i'm out here.
doing reckless ass shit.
sleeping w/ no scarf.

gets 'turn that cherry out' tattooed on my inner thigh

i am new new from "atl"
i am ronnie from "the player's club"
i am ursula in "set it off"
i am keisha in "belly"
i am isis in "bring it on"
i am akasha in "queen of the damned"
i am yvette in "baby boy"

shows up to ur wedding w/ micro braids, glowing skin, snatched eyebrows, a red jersey dress, and manolo blahnik timbs

shoutout to me for wearing the same shit for like 2 years.

i'm not gone put any typa concealer under my eyes no more because the lil baggies and dark circles under my eyes add a lil character to my face. they make me look like i then been thru some thangs AND I HAVE.

When I was younger, I used to want to be that little black girl on the just for me perm box.

shoutout to my homie God for giving me this fat ass and this beautiful brown skin.

pulls up in a lil ice blue mercedes
steps out in a lil vintage fubu jersey dress
takes my red lollipop outta my mouth for a lil min
ties up the strings of my manolo blahnik timbaland boots
applies more gel to my baby hairs
watches u hoes turn green wit envy

18

reapplies lipstick after i finish sucking dick

makes my pussy pumpkin spice flavored for the fall

no offense but i'm happy as hell that i'm a black woman.

#TeamILook16WithoutMakeUpOn

kionna taking out her lollipop to suck tommy's dick in the movie 'belly' is my aesthetic! i can go from innocent and playful to a lil freak hoe in like 5 seconds.

can only express my emotions thru emojis

babygirl/hoodrat checklist:
she got a tatt on her ankle!
she got the chinese slipper joints from the beauty store.
she still live w/ her momma but she be sneaking niggas in her bedroom.
she got a gold ankle bracelet w/ her name on it, matching necklace, and the matching earrings.
she thinks all niggas ain't shit but she still deal w/ em on some type of level.
Trina lyrics are scripture.
she goes to school and does hair on the side from time to time.
she got zebra print or cheetah print on the steering wheel and seats of her car.
she's gotten into numerous fights w/ bitches that wanted to test her.
she once held her boyfriend's coke in her bra while the cops searched their apartment.
she lied for her nigga in court.
her favorite saying is 'run up get done up'
she ain't got a tumblr.
her favorite movie is 'baby boy'
her nails are ALWAYS 3 inches or longer.
she got a lollipop or gum in her mouth 85% of the time.

still crying @ the fact that I can never be a 90's r&b superstar.

i am truly team
#noMatterhowMuchSleepIgetThereWillAlwaysBeLilBaggiesUndaMy
EyesBecauseIBeenThruSomeThangs

adjusts glasses according to a recent study, the bitches wit the worse eyesight got the best pussy.

looks betta than all the people that lied 2 me and did me wrong

everytime i listen to jealoUs.Mp3 by Beyoncé, i pretend that i'm a passive aggressive housewife sitting in the dark wearing a vintage Balenciaga gown drinking a glass of wine out the bottle waiting for my drunk emotionally detached husband who has community dick but hasn't made love to me in months to come home from the club.

fall aesthetic:
one titty out
burgundy lips
a glass of wine in one hand

nothing says 2002 like a velour tracksuit honestly.

#TeamPettyAndPretty

looks at my best selfies on my off days to remind myself that i'm still a bad bitch

i'm going to be a
care free black cutie for 2014.
hbu?

sucking lollipops around niggas while maintaining eye contact with them
#littleHoeThings

stabs a hoe for a lisa frank backpack

catch me up in da produce aisle deciding which fruit is ripe or not.

if i'm not rolling my eyes in response to everything
i'm not alive

gets baby girl tattooed on my ankle

shea butter, coconut oil, a beauty blender, a lifetime supply of gum, a glowing complexion, a personal trainer, a lifetime supply of baby wipes, a huge ass water bottle, a makeup artist, 2 bundles of virgin hair, an aloe vera plant, nipple piercings, belly button piercing, a diamond choker, a diamond ankle bracelet, and a hood nigga.

#TeamImNot15yrsOldIJustLookItBlackDontCrackEternalYouthFuckWitMe

naaaaa na na na
wait til i get my sew in bitch
in my kanye west voice

u ask me to be a bridesmaid at ur wedding

shows up in a blue fubu jersey and manolo blank timberland boots instead of the ugly ass dress u wanted me to wear

#TeamGrownWomanWithABabyFace

this summer will be all about
overalls against bare skin
laid baby hair
lollipops
big curly ass hair
jelly sandals
crop tops
sheer tops that expose a lil nipple
ankle bracelets
denim crop tops
lucite heels
gold accessories
belly chains
high waisted jean shorts

opens flip phone to check my messages

bends over to tie up the strings on my Manolo Blahnik timbs
gels my edges down
hops in my ice blue mercedes convertible
checks my eyebrows in the mirror

takes my gum out to give u the suck up

my outfit could be really shitty but if my face game and my hair game is on point it don't even matter that much. it does but it don't.

i am.
I am the purple pasty lil kim wore at the 1999 mtv video music awards.
i am nelly's band aid.
i am the pink velour tracksuit jennifer lopez wore in the "i'm real" remix music video.
i am ashanti's sideburns.
i am Mariah Carey's whistle notes.
i am the bellychain aaliyah wore in the "Are You That Somebody" music video.
i am Andre 3000's mole.
i am the versace dress Beyoncé wore in the "crazy in love" music video.
i am.

only invites u to chill so u can see how good my eyebrows look

from cutie to bad bitch: a come up story

1. take ur shirt off
2. take ur bra off
3. play jay z's 'change clothes'
4. walk across whatever room ur in like it's a runway
5. stomp the floor and let ur titties bounce on the beat
6. look in the mirror and say 'ima bad bitch today'

i live for the futuristic vibes of r&b videos in the early 2000s like the black leather, the corny special effects, the dance breaks, i live for it all.

i fully support sneakers w/ dresses looks!

pink velour tracksuit
Gold hoop earrings
manolo blahnik timbaland boots
afro puffs
Gold ankle bracelet
pink motorola razor flip phone

easy breezy beautiful brown bad bitch <3

NIGGAS

A NIGGA THAT'S OLDER THAN ME.
A NIGGA THAT AIN'T GOT NO TYPA SOCIAL NETWORKING SITES.
A NIGGA THAT KNOWS HOW AMAZING I AM.
A NIGGA THAT EATS PUSSY JUST FOR THE SAKE OF EATING PUSSY
NOT JUST TO GET IT WET SO HE CAN STICK HIS DICK IN IT.
A NIGGA THAT'S LIKE 8 FEET.
A NIGGA THAT CONSISTENTLY GETS FRESH ASS LINE UPS.
A NIGGA THAT SAYS SOME FUNNY ASS SHIT THAT WILL HAVE ME
UGLY LAUGHING.
A NIGGA THAT BUYS ME SHIT.
A NIGGA THAT CAN TEACH ME SHIT AND I CAN HOLD A DEEP
MEANINGFUL CONVERSATION WIT.
A NIGGA THAT IS EMOTIONALLY MATURE.
A NIGGA THAT IS NOT AFRAID TO SHOW ME OFF TO HIS MAMA.
A NIGGA THAT WILL PUT ME OVA HIS HOMIES.
A NIGGA THAT IS STILL ATTRACTED TO ME WHEN I AIN'T GOT MA
WEAVE IN.
A NIGGA THAT DOESN'T STAN FOR TRASH ASS RAPPERS.
A NIGGA THAT IS NOT TRANSPHOBIC OR MISOGYNISTIC.
A NIGGA THAT WILL HELP ME GROW AND PROGRESS AND LOVE
MYSELF MORE THAN I ALREADY DO.
A NIGGA THAT DOESN'T ACTUALLY TALK SHIT ABOUT BLACK
WOMEN.
A NIGGA THAT'S NOT ON SOME RESPECTABILITY ASHY ANKH
NIGGA SHIT.
A NIGGA THAT WILL WRITE POETRY ABOUT HOW GOOD MY ASS
LOOKS AND HOW GOOD MY TITTIES LOOK.
A NIGGA THAT CARES ABOUT MY NUT MORE THAN HIS NUT.
A DARK SKIN NIGGA.
A HOOD ASS NIGGA.
A NIGGA WITH PROMINENT ARM VEINS.
A NIGGA WIT A MOTORCYCLE SO I CAN RIDE AROUND THE CITY
WIT HIM WHILE MY HAIR BLOW IN THE WIND.
A NIGGA THAT LOOKS AT ME LIKE JA RULE LOOKED AT ASHANTI
IN THE MESMERIZE MUSIC VIDEO WHEN SHE STEPPED OUT IN THE
ALL BLACK JOINT.
A NIGGA THAT IS NOT AFRAID TO SHOW EMOTION OR
VULNERABILITY.

*

don't congratulate these niggas for doing the basics!!!!!!!! make these niggas work for u and go above and beyond because ur worth nothing less!! the next nigga that's tryna get w/ me gotta bring me some dust from the planet mars in a cup and be willing to take me on late night motorcycle rides when eva i ask him to!

skinny niggas have the biggest dicks. never underestimate a skinny ass nigga. that's all i'm saying.

i'm a huge fan of niggas that grab me by the waist from behind and niggas that have me ugly laughing.

it's 2014 and u niggas are still sending lame ass ashy dick pics and expecting us to be impressed like???

the worst thing a nigga can take from u is T I M E.

niggas really be out here justifying their shitty doo doo ass behavior on their childhood or circumstances in their life! naw nigga! don't play the victim! just because u had a shitty life growing up as a young shawty or u got issues in ur life rn doesn't give u the license to cheat, lie, or be a shitty ass person! the fuck!!!!

it rly irritates me when niggas bash thin black girls or when they say shit like "she ain't got no ass" ..."she's not thick enough". meanwhile, they be having little ashy dicks.

if a nigga is only giving u like 5 seconds of foreplay....get out. leave that relationship ma because he don't care about u. he in it for HISSELF.

i want a nigga that can teach me a coupla thangs and he's actually about shit! like let's discuss deep shit. let's exchange a meaningful conversation that i think about years from now! expand my knowledge! don't just talk about how much u wanna fuck or how u finna fix up yo ride! let's get deeper than that bae!!!!!! B L O W M E A W A Y.

never fuck a nigga with a dirty car! if he can't maintain a clean car, u dealing with a crusty ass nigga who don't care about nothing in life! save urself the trouble!!!!

some niggas are soooo dumb. they tell u cute romantic shit but then will turn around and say 'i don't want a relationship'. they'll flirt and thirst over other bitches but then will get so angry when they even think ur talking to another nigga.

let's be real for a min! if a nigga says some corny ass shit like 'i wanna be with u but i don't like labels on our relationship', he is using that as an excuse to fuck otha hoes but still keep u around. STAY WOKE.

niggas who make u feel like a grown woman and a little girl at the same time are the best. whea the niggas who tryna give my grown ass a piggy back ride and throw me in the air like i weigh 10 pounds or some shit???

i'm fucking heated that niggas really think that women who wear weaves are 'not being real' and are 'self hating' and all that other bullshit. the way a woman chooses to wear her hair is none of ur fucking concern. i'm so fucking sick of u niggas slamming women who wear weaves or women that choose to relax their hair! this shit is so stupid!!!!!! just because lil mama got her brazilian weave in w/ a closure doesn't mean she loves herself any less than the mami w/ the fro!!!!!!!!!

why do black women get weave instead of rocking their own God given natural hair? why are black women out here twerking instead of getting their degree? why are black women so concerned with shows such as basketball wives and love and hip hop? i want a black woman with class. i'm tired of thots. i don't know about ya'll but i want a black queen so i can be her black king. -a typical ashy ankh nigga

hood niggas go for the quiet low-key nerdy cute bitch in the back of the class room with the curly hair and drawings in ha notebook!

If you gotta pretend to be interested in sports to keep a nigga's interest, then you're a wack ass bitch.

they don't want u to love urself too much. they want u to second guess ya self a lil bit. they don't want u to gas yo own self up. niggas want u to need them a lil bit.

ima start holding u niggas to the same unrealistic standards that ya'll hold us women to. u want a bad bitch wit a 20 inch waist and no stretch marks? well i want a nigga with a 6 pack and no baby mama.

a scientific study reveals that niggas who have anything negative to say about black women be ugly as shit 99.9% of the time.

takes a sip of green tea dealing with niggas can be so exhausting fr. like no one wants to take a bitch out anymore or buy a bitch something. niggas stay wanting to fuck and 'chill' and i'm so over that? like? bitch i understand not having money and shit because fuck i'm a college student i be broke sometimes too but got damn. niggas don't want to pay for nothing but want u to do all types of shit for them and idgi? like? all these niggas are so lame. they don't want a relationship with u but they will foam at the mouth at the idea of fucking u. they don't want u but they stay asking "who u on the phone with?" and other types of possessive ass bullshit questions. OF COURSE I'M TALKING TO OTHA NIGGAS. LIKE DUH. *they don't want u but they don't want another nigga to have u. and all of this nonsense is so wild to me. niggas are so selfish and childish. like grow up and stop playing around all the damn time. let a bitch know whether u tryna get serious or not. i sometimes worry that i'll never come across a nigga that wants to claim me in a genuine way. that doesn't just wanna fuck and have a casual situation going on. but whateva. at the end of the day i still have me. *washes out my mug* *puts mug in the dish washer**

dear coon ass niggas, stop giving white hoes a pass to say nigga just because they are fucking ur corny ass.

don't hesitate to eliminate any nigga out of ur life that makes u second guess urself for even one moment.

niggas: why she dressed like that? don't she got respect for herself? man she out there! look at that smut! no one ever gonna wife that bitch! she out here giving pussy to any and every nigga. I bet this bitch's body count outta this world fam!!!!!! hahahhahaha!!!!!! ball is life! u gotta take a bitch swimmin on the first date!!!!! i love women wit no makeup! yo bitches be lookin crazy wit that bright colored lipstick! especially the dark ones!!!! hahahaha!!!!!!! i hate weave! be real! take out that weave!!!!! don't ask me to take u no where hoe because i ain't spending a dime on u!!!!!! come over to my crib tho girl!!!!! my momma not home so i can fuck all day!!!!!! i wanna fuck raw bitch!!!!! RAWWWWW! U KNOW A NIGGA CAN'T FEEL NO PUSSY WEARIN A RUBBA! I WANNA FEEELLL DAT PUSSY. BALL IS LIFE!!!!!! *lemme hold 30 dollars tho and i got u on friday when i get paid! Can i borrow ya* car for a coupla days? my car fucked up! can u share my mix tape on twitter baby? u got more followers than me and i need them to see it so they can download it. u like my song right? u fuck wit it right? my nigga say he gotta better verse than me but i think i bodied that nigga hahahah!!!!! man i was up in walmart the otha day and i saw this bitch that had the most saggiest titties fam! them shits was sweepin the floor!!!!! i'm glad yo titties ain't like that ma! MAN THESE BITCHES DON'T BE LOYAL I SWEA FAM. YEAH I BE DOIN FOUL SHIT FROM TIME TO TIME BUT IF SHE LOVE ME SHE CAN'T GIVE UP ON A NIGGA LIKE THAT YA FEEL ME? BABY GIRL AIN'T A RIDE OR DIE. SHE DON'T CARE ABOUT A NIGGA. i mean we ain't togetha or nothin like that because i'm coolin right nah but i'm feelin her! she better not be fuckin otha niggas tho! that's my pussy! BALL IS LIFE!!!!!! ME AND MY NIGGAS REAL ALL DAY EVERYDAY! but anyways like i was sayin i can fuck otha bitches but she can't fuck otha niggas. that's fucked up. that's breakin the code bruh. she know that pussy belong to me. she know i be diggin in them guts. anyway i just gotta text fam! lemme go see if this hoe down the street tryna give a nigga the suck up. BALL IS LIFE!!!!!

don't hold ur farts in for NO nigga.

u niggas would cave if u received even a fraction of the criticism a black woman receives every fucking day.

i'm sick of niggas that talk about sex all the time!!!!!!!!!!!! grow up!!!!!!!!!!!

a recent study confirms that 3 out of 4 niggas ain't shit.

shoutout to the niggas that use the same towel they wipe their ass with as their face towel.
shoutout to the niggas that reblog nothing but skinny lightskin bitches and weed all fucking day long.
shoutout to the niggas that's having phone sex rn bc they can't get pussy irl.
shoutout to the niggas that's about to send a bitch an ashy pic of their dick rn.
shoutout to the niggas that's fucking with timbs on.
shoutout to the niggas that's beating their meat to twerking videos on youtube.
shoutout to the lame ass darkskin niggas that clown on darkskin females bc hey're insecure about their own fucking color.

i can't stand 'what will white ppl think of us?? ur embarrassing us as black people. the black community gotta do better!' type niggas! WHO THE FUCK CARES WHAT A CRACKER THINKS????

always pay attention to how a nigga deals with u being angry with him. see if he reaches out to u to try to make things right again or if he acts distant and non chalant as fuck.

never let a nigga dim ur light or make u feel ashamed for complimenting urself or biggin urself up. like don't let a nigga make u question ur greatness or make u feel like ur acting 'entitled' for wanting to be treated with respect.

never trust a nigga w/ dirty ass fingernails. a nigga w/ dirty fingernails don't love himself therefore he will never love you.

shoutout to the niggas who still think we have our makeup on point, our hair done, and our outfits on point solely for their eyes to see. that we wake up in the morning and say to ourselves "what nigga can i impress today."

every single nigga i have ever talked to got a mixtape in the works.

if ur playing suga mama to a nigga that's not doing shit for u then you need to reevaluate your entire life.

niggas who complain about 'saggy' titties ain't neva seen a bitch naked irl. grow up. gravity is a real concept. like???? not every pair of titties u see is going to be perky and sittin up. G R O W U P.

niggas who don't want to be ya bae but want bae privileges are the worst typa niggas.

i will forever side eye niggas who will go out of their way to gas up a mediocre white girl over a black girl.

niggas are so fucking fake. they will tell u 'oh i love all types of women' but will have a blog full of mixed bitches.

there's nothing worse than a nigga that only looks cute w/ a fitted on. he take off that shit and ur like wooooooooooow.

the best revenge against a nigga that did u wrong is stuntin on him. looking so fucking good that he wished he had another shot with u. making more money than him! making sure ur edges are in tact! making sure u getting a good night's rest! making sure u ain't lurking on his insta or twitter! being content with being alone! making sure u get that 64 ounces of water intake everyday! u can prosper without that nigga!!!!!

beware of those 'when u getting ur weave back in baby?' ass niggas

beware of those 'why u wearing that crazy ass color lipstick?' ass niggas

beware of those 'what did she do to get beat so badly?' ass niggas

beware of those 'ew that bitch is fat' ass niggas

beware of those 'dark skin bitches with blonde hair look like duracell batteries' ass niggas

beware of those 'that little girl is a thot!' ass niggas

beware of those niggas that say misogynistic ass shit. beware of those niggas that say transphobic shit. don't let them slide just because they are ur boyfriend, ur friend, ur father, ur uncle or whatever. call them out on their bullshit. Hold them accountable for the bullshit that they say.

niggas who go on and on about how 'real' they are be the fakest niggas. like why u trying so hard to convince me u real :/ like?

if he don't have a case on his phone
that mean he be fucking bitches raw!

talk about another nigga in front of ur boy and if he don't get mad or jealous, he never cared about yo ass and he never will.

any nigga that still loves u when ur hair is fucked up, u got pimples or scars on ur face, u don't have a flat stomach, or on days u don't look ur best appearance wise is the typa nigga to keep around!

mediocre niggas have to be reminded of shit they are supposed to do. i need a nigga that already knows the right shit to do without me having to utter a word.

u niggas really gotta stop putting women into two categories, smut and wife material....like that's so insulting. Honestly, women are so much more complex and dynamic than that! most men are so weak that they get so scared or uncomfortable when they see a bad bitch in control of her sexuality and knows what she want outta life. like just because i like to do freaky hoe shit doesn't mean i'm not a good person or nurturing or loyal or honest.

i don't trust niggas that don't like tupac.

dealing w/ niggas is like
picking change up off the floor w/ 3 inch acrylic nails.

niggas be wanting bitches wit crazy unrealistic body measurements like 40-12-85 but have the audacity to have small ashy dicks :/

how do fake ass niggas even get sleep at night? like???

me: i am literally deleting this nigga's numba and blocking him foreva! fuck i look like dealing wit his bullshit! i am too cute for this! like who the fuck do this nigga think he is!!!!!!!!! FUCK THIS SHIT!!!!!! i'm thru! done! finished! IMA FALL THE FUCK BACK FOREVA.
him: hey
me: omg hey boo wussup!!!!! what's good!

shoutout to the niggas who aren't afraid to moan when they are getting fucked or getting sucked!

some of ya'll niggas have a million requirements for women but the minute we have height requirements for ya'll, ya'll feelings are hurt.

l00k, i would date a broke nigga honestly but he gotta have some typa ambition? like he can't be comfortable with being br0ke? he gotta have some typa hustle and he gotta be on the come up and he can't be on no social networks flexin like he got shit when he really don't. we can hustle together bae and build an empire but u gotta be on the grind. u can't be playing video games in yo underwear at yo mama's house waiting for life to happen 2 u. u gotta be out making some typa moves. i don't expect niggas to be rich but i do expect niggas to have some typa hunger to want better for themselves. ya feel me?

If he can't deal with ur stretchmarks, ur belly fat, ur body hair, or the fact that ur pussy doesn't smell like flowers then u dealing with a lil baby ass nigga. a nigga that complains about shit like that ain't use to getting any typa pussy or ain't never seen a bitch naked. We don't complain about y'all pot bellies, the fact that ur balls hairy as shit or ur receding hairlines

how many hoes have u said this 2 = my thoughts when a nigga is tryna flirt wit me.

complains that niggas ain't shit but still continue to deal with them on some typa level only because i love the attention they give

shoutout to the niggas that's eating ass for the first time rn.
shoutout to the niggas that's buying shit they can't afford rn.
shoutout to the niggas that busting a nut right now as i'm typing this.

niggas love to ask questions like who u on the phone wit? who was that calling u? where u at? who u chilling wit? when ur paying my bills and giving me good dick then MAYBE u can worry about all of that.

THIS NIGGA AIN'T SHIT. I SWEA I AIN'T NEVA TALKING TO THIS MUTHA…..
phone rings
answers it
OH HEY BABY!! HOW WAS UR DAY?

my favorite pasttime is catching a nigga in a lie.

niggas: i want a bad bitch wit a 22 inch waist! she gotta have long hair too! no weave! i need her to be mixed wit something too! can't have my babies comin out all dark and crispy bruh! she gotta have a huge fat ass and she can't love herself too much! she also can't expect me to take her ass out anywhere because i ain't buying that bitch shit! i ain't tryna have a hoe take all my fucking money! fuck i look like?!!! money ova bitches! my niggas over any hoe! ball is life! that hoe betta know how to cook something too! can't have a nigga starving and shit. she betta *know how to throw dat ass back in the bedroom too! i want a bitch that's gone suck me up for hours and hours but ima lick her pussy for like 6 seconds to get her a lil wet so i can put my dick in it hahahaha! oh and she better shave that shit too! nigga can't deal wit no hair all up in my mouth! but she better lick these hairy ass balls tho! hahahahahahaha ball is life! BALL IS LIFE!!!! okay bye finna send everyone on twitta dot com a link to my mix tape and annoy the fuck out of everybody and play ball wit my niggas! bye ya'll. peace. BALL IS LIFE.*

niggas want pussy but won't even buy a bitch a hamburger. fuck outta here.

90%of the time crusty OLD niggas that are old enough to be my father spit game at me and then there's 10% of the time when niggas that's decent looking and actually my age spits game. is God trying to tell me something??????

nigga, if u approach me wearing open toed shoes, u then already lost bruh. pack ur shit and go home. it's over.

selfish niggas do shit like lick ur pussy for exactly 2.5 seconds and expect u to suck them off for like 5 hours. selfish niggas do shit like have side bitches but then get mad when u even glance at a nigga in public. selfish niggas do shit like expect u to pay their phone bill while they on the phone chatting it up with numerous hoes. selfish niggas do shit like thirst and jack off to instagram pics but get angry when he see u like one nigga's pic. selfish niggas do shit like borrow ur car for a day and pick up otha bitches in it. don't deal with a selfish nigga. please don't sis, it ain't worth it.

grown niggas don't care whether u shaved down there or not!!!!

ways to know if ur stuck or sprung on a nigga
u have opportunities for new dick but u only want his
u travel for his dick
u see his name on yo phone and u get lowkey excited as fuck but act all non chalant when u answer the phone
u secretly stalk his ass on social networking sites checking to see if he checking for other bitches
he says some cute shit to u and u try to front and play like u don't give a shit but ur clit is flip flopping and ur smiling crazy hard and shit
just one touch or kiss from this nigga is like getting electrical shock

ur crazy jealous if u see him give another bitch any ounce of the attention he gives to u
u roll ur eyes and say shit like 'boy bye' to him (u don't want him to know he got ur ass sprung lowkey so u act like u don't give a fuck)
u think about his dick sliding in u in class

niggas who only talk about sex are so boring and lame. like tell me what's ur fav color. what's ur fav tv show and why? what games u used to play as a lil shawty? i don't want to hear u tryna sell me ur dick game the whole time we talking. shit.

a fuck boy
complains about stretch marks or pubic hair
his tumblr archive is a sea of racially ambiguous women and pictures of weed
expects u to suck him up for like 5 hours but eats u out for like 2 seconds
his twitter and instagram is full of transphobic ana misogynistic shit
he does music and it's garbage but he swears that he got bars
he texts u shit like 'when u gone see me?' or 'send me a pic'
he got that fuck boy hair cut

be wary of niggas who only notice ya when ya weave in.

if ur feeling urself getting thirsty over a nigga
pls conceal it
because once these niggas know u sweatin em just a little bit
that's when they show the fuck out.

i don't trust any nigga with an instagram account.

i used to be into niggas that were assholes but now that i'm older i'm so over that?! like i want a nigga that's not ashamed to admit they are into u! a nigga that is very self aware! a nigga that society would deem thirsty! a nigga that's not gonna let no one say some wild shit about u when u ain't around. a loyal 'ima fuck u instead of hanging out with my niggas tonight' typa nigga!!!! niggas that act too fucking cool for that shit are corny and lame!

do i actually like this nigga or am i loving the attention he gives me: a memoir by me

ima need u niggas to stop defining 'good hair' as a loose curl pattern.
'good hair' is healthy hair. plain and simple.

some of the same niggas that scream 'shave it' when it comes to pussy are the same
niggas that don't wash their balls for a week. pls spare meeeeeee.

some niggas be doing mad deceitful wild shit like getting their dick sucked by
anotha bitch while talking to their fiancé on the phone or will lie multiple times
without feeling no typa way about it but these same fake ass niggas be having the
nerve to say shit like 'why are ya'll females so bitter?' 'we all ain't like dat
shawty'.....or my favorite! 'i just need a girl i can trust' like if ya'll don't sit ya'll
fake corny asses down somewhere!

pay attention to a nigga's actions. that's how they really feel.

Never letting these niggas stress me out is the only anti aging regimen I'll ever be
on.

ugly niggas treat u like ur the second coming of christ.
pretty niggas treat u like shit.

can someone pls explain to me
why niggas are so scared and terrified of marriage
but have the audacity to be bold and brave when it comes
to nutting in bitches and fucking bitches raw?

nigga i swallowed ur babies. the least u could do is text me back in a
timely manner.

shoutout to the niggas that say they love all black girls of any shade and then will
turn around and say dark skin girls don't look good wearing

_____.

God gave me the gift of discernment so that i can easily determine the difference between a real nigga and a fake nigga.

if u texting a nigga and telling him u just ate and if he says some shit like 'damn bae! u ain't save me none?' he's a corny ass nigga.

if that nigga got u comparing urself to other girls and stressed out about what he may or may not be doing then pls let him go! it ain't worth it!!!!!! THESE NIGGAS ARE REPLACEABLE.

when i ask a nigga how old he is i be praying silently that he either my age or older because i can't deal with young niggas. i'm too m a t u r e.

takes a sip out of my water bottle i often worry that i will never have sex comfortably with a boy. like all the sexual encounters i have had with niggas have been really unsatisfying and awkward because niggas don't believe in foreplay or making a bitch feel good anymore. they just care about they nut. i want a nigga to take his time with me and slowly undress me and stare at my body for like 5 hours before he even touches it and then touch it for like 13 hours and write poetry about how good my titties look and how soft my ass is and then eat my pussy for like 8 hours then suck on each titty for like 4 hours each and then kiss me for like 2 hours and then he can finally stick his dick in. it's very outrageous to me that niggas will expect a suck up but aren't willing to eat it? like who the fuck do u think u are? like if i'm not dripping like a river then don't even fucking bother. put ya dick away boy. lol.

i love it when ur sucking a nigga up and u can see the veins about to pop out of his forehead as he's trying to focus on that nut. he tryna hide it in his face how good that shit feels. then he moans like a little bitch when he finally bust.

thinks about dick at work
thinks about dick at school
thinks about dick all the got damn time

him: **takes his dick out**
me: *my momma said i gotta go home rn.*

i'll neva fall victim to white boy thirst.

i love niggas too much.

me: omg these niggas ain't shit!!! i swea!!!!! i'm done fucking with these niggas!
ima wife myself up!

me: omg i get to see da bae 2nite!

*doesn't give u any pussy because i saw u smoking a cigarette a while ago and i
knew u didn't love yo self so u can't possibly love me and my pussy*

I love having my ass grabbed so much like especially if a nigga is aggressive with
it? Like??? BiTch when he hit u with that grab and smack combo!!!!!
Bitchhhhhhh when he squeeze yo booty meat so hard that u feel like u might just
black out! And bitch don't get me started on when a nigga's hands rub ur ass in
a circular type motion! Like pls!!!!!!! And bitch when u walking away to
leave...the last lil smack he give yo booty!!!!! Toss it, flip it, grab it, smack it!!!

shoutout to the boys that actually stan for their girlfriend and aren't afraid to
show it!!!!!! keep posting pics of ur girl, keep saying u love and adore ha! keep
showing her attention and affection! keep treating her with respect! let her know
that she's a bad bitch and that u think she's perfect! keep sending lil cute text
messages! keep giving ha flowers! love is so cute honestly!!!

THIS IS SUPER CORNY BUT um i cannot wait until i talk to a nigga
that's not just wanting to fuck me? that actually wants to talk about other things
with me and he values my opinions and my views on shit and sees me as an actual
human being instead of a moist hole he can stick his dick into? and i honestly be
wanting a relationship sometimes. but i don't want a nigga wanting to get with me
based on how i look but i want someone to want to get with me based on the fact
that i'm fucking amazing and they don't want another nigga to scoop me up. they
gotta have me now and get me off the market so no one else can typa thing? and i
want a nigga to actually listen to the songs i like and watch the movies that i like
and tell me what color should i get for my next manicure and which fubu jersey
color would look best. and i want him to cry in front of me and be vulnerable and
show me his emotional side and lay in my arms like he's a fucking infant and shit
and i just hold him and comfort him while we listen to neptunes instrumentals
and sit in silence reflecting ana contemplating on how we found each other and
how long this shit will last....OMG I'M SO CORNY.

i like arguments low-key because that's when the tru nature of a nigga comes out. when ya'll arguing, u truly get an idea about how much he cares about u! whether he'll call u back if u hang up on him or how he deals with u being angry.i live for the #Drama of it all. it's boring as hell being with a nigga u never argue with!!!!! what's the fucking fun in that?!

have u ever just wanted to do some corny but cute ass shit like hold a nigga's hand and just sit in ur car with him listening to neptunes instrumentals and bops from the late 90's and early 2000s for a coupla hours as the sun is going down and randomly kiss him not in a 'i wanna fuck u' way but in a 'wow i really like u' typa way???

hood nigga checklist:

he lives w/ his grandma or aunt.

he ain't got no typa social networking site.

he refers to u as 'ma' 'babygirl' or 'shawty'.

he gotta gun.

he tatted the fuck up.

he sells drugs or has sold drugs in the past.

if a nigga grabs me by the waist or tickles me ima giggle and push em away but low-key my stomach is going crazy and my clit feels like it does when I'm riding down a steep hill in the whip.

one of my fav moments in life is when ur making out with a nigga and it feels so good to have him kissing u and gripping ur booty meat that u feel dizzy and delirious and his mouth and body is the only thing that matters to u in that lil moment and u so consumed with this nigga that u feel like u gone pass out.

first date ideas: u eating my pussy til it's numb

let me brush yo waves babe. lemme braid ur hair on the front porch. lemme suck that dick at the movie theatre. lemme take care of u.

hmu if u cute, like 7 feet tall, got dreads or a fresh ass fade, look like u sell cocaine, or u look like u then been thru some thangs.

there is something so fucking sexy
about a goofy ass nigga.
like where are the niggas that will have me in tears from laughter?

can the science side of tumbla dot com tell me why am i so attracted to hood ass
niggas that look like they been thru a coupla thangs and sold a coupla thangs?
notify a bitch like please?

i am a huge fan of:

niggas that will have me crying because they are so fucking funny

niggas that actually have good hygiene

tall niggas

ugly but in a cute kind of way niggas

hood niggas

niggas with prominent veins in their arms and hands

niggas who actually tell the truth and don't lie about petty shit

niggas w/ no social networks :)

wants a turbulent relationship with lots of fighting and makeup sex
wants a peaceful relationship with no drama
loves drama lowkey

i love it when a nigga grabs my waist from behind and i can feel his shit pressed
all on my ass.

hmu if u cute and u don't play video games or u don't watch sports and u stay
home alot and never go out so u can give all of ur attention to important shit that
matters : me

i love it when a nigga is sucking ur titties and he is so passionate about it!!! like? he closing his eyes and shit like he is nursing or sumn and he moving his head in a circular motion just cherishing the hell out of ur titty and sucking it like it's not gonna be there tomorrow. nigga be taking like 20 min for each titty and u just watching him and living for it. he bite it and nibble on it and u just feel like u gone die a lil bit. the way a nigga sucks ur titty is a prelude to how he's gonna eat ur pussy honestly.

i miss hugging a tall ass nigga and just feeling like a grown woman and a little girl at the same time.

i miss kissing and touching and being held and shit. not on some freaky ass shit. but on some cute shit.

i miss being wanted.

lowkey
i think it's super cute when
niggas sing songs in a high pitched 'girly' tone of voice.
or try to immitate or copy my voice in a joking way.
that shit makes me laugh everytime.

i love it when niggas touch me in unexpected places like my hair or behind my ear and don't just go for the erogenous zones right away like animals. it's so cute.

when ur in the mood for some dick but don't want to deal with the nigga that the dick is attached to.

i wish a boy would draw a picture of me or write me a song! i'm a corny ass bitch but i love little cute innocent shit like that! i get so bored of niggas that only tell me how much they want to fuck me? like duh? I'm cute as hell. what else is new?

if u a boy and i eva told u to square up and i threatened to beat ur ass in a playful lil way then i'm feelin u.

nigga if i sucked ur dick u better kiss me in the fucking mouth afterwards....tongue and all! why u so scared of ur own got damn body fluids? like????

shoutout to the niggas that actually appreciate lingerie when u got it on before ya'll about to get down to business instead of ripping it off u like a wild animal.

i don't care how good a nigga looks or how amazing his stroke game is, he will never be allowed to treat me like shit. i love myself before i love any of these niggas.

i'm allergic to fuck niggas!

shoutout to my niggas that stay strong and continue to live their life when none of these hoes won't let em
and shoutout to my niggas that still carry on even tho they are constantly being slept on.

me: i'm tired of being a hoe. i think i'm ready 2 be a wife.
*me: *sees fine ass nigga wit honey colored dreads**
me: wow i wonder how my manicure would look clawing into his back when he beating dat thang up.

boys who are not afraid to be vulnerable and show emotion are honestly my fav? like i want bae to cry in front of me and let go and #losehimself

rolls my eyes when a nigga says something cute 2 me

shoutout to boys who text song lyrics. ya'll are cute and rare.

an aggressive nigga that takes control is honestly all i need because i feel like i have to be in control all the time and it's nice to let someone else be in control for once.

tall niggas are so adorable because while hugging them u feel so safe and small in their arms and plus u don't have to bend down as far to suck em' up. it's a win/win.

but for real tho, shoutout to the dark skin boys with nice ass lips!!!

i know i'm over a nigga when:
i don't check his social networking sites looking for any signs that he's talking to hoes
i block him or delete his numba
i'm not jealous anymore!!!!
i never talk about him anymore to my homegirls

my hugs are different w/ niggas that i like and niggas that i don't like. like if i'm feeling u like that, i'm going to make sure i press my breasts against ur chest when we hug. but if i'm not really into u like that, ima give u an awkward side hug and a small pat on the back.

turn around and walk away from me if u ain't over 6 feet and u ain't got nice lips.

i'm so fickle. like one day i would be wanting a nigga then the next i'm on some me myself and i fuck these niggas type shit.

if he got a case on his iPhone and his screen ain't cracked, he got some good dick.

LOOK if i have feelings for u, my clit gone jump and flip flop everytime u say some cute ass shit to me.

if we go together ion want u talking to another bitch, complimenting another bitch's picture, liking another bitch's picture, chilling w/ another bitch etc etc. the fuck i look like sharing dick w/ another bitch?! you got me all the way fucked up. i'm the only bitch in yo life besides yo momma. you don't need nobody else nigga.

the three commandments <3

commandment 1: thou shalt not be pressed over a nigga that ain't urs.

commandment 2: thou shalt not let any of these niggas make u feel any type of way about urself.

commandment 3: thou shalt not put dick over ur homegirls or girl crew. they were there before ur nigga. they'll be there after.

my only regret in life is letting a nigga make me question my beauty and greatness.

bruh, it feels sooo good when the level of thirst is mutual.

lemme brush yo waves on the front porch bae while all the hoes that's envious of our love watch us and glare as they walk by #HoodLove

sext: send me a pic of yo fresh ass line up bae

if he got polo boxers, he got some good dick. if he got hanes, the dick is trash.

have u eva been addicted to the way a nigga looks at u?

*i could do a 5 page essay on how important
tall niggas are*

if we kissing and u not grabbing that booty meat, i'll never talk to 2 u again.

**sees da bae pull up wit a fresh line up*
immediately gets wet
*calls the cops**

makes a nigga wait half a century for some pussy

i love it when ur kissing a nigga and u can feel his facial hair tickle u a lil bit.

hood niggas that say please and thank u.

saying 'boy shut up' and rolling my eyes is my fav way of flirting with niggas!

i think it's so cute when a nigga shows off his girl on a social network!

fetish: niggas wit fresh line ups

i really can't deal with no nigga treating me in a non chalant typa way because i'm amazing and i'm the perfect bitch. like i don't completely have my shit together yeah yeah whatever but i'm a lil cutie and i'm laid-back yet kind of mysterious and complicated. i'm a lil low-key typa shawty. i just be peeping shit out quietly and i have great taste in music and my ass is soft. and i don't ask for nothing but all of ur attention.

even when u niggas sleep on me, i'm woke on my own self. i know how great i am. i know i'm a gem.

i want someone that is on my level mentally so much. i'm not saying be boring and serious all the time because that's boring as fuck but don't be vapid and goofy all the fucking time like??? i want to have some grown ass conversations about shit that's important. shit that matters. i want to be challenged mentally. i want someone that's going to make me think about shit from a different perspective. i crave meaningful conversation. i want to be taught a coupla thangs.

God please prepare my pussy for this dick i am about to receive. let my walls stretch like my 4c hair stretches after a fresh twist out. give me the strength to handle this nigga's stroke game. let me not turn away from this blessing. let me receive it with open legs so that i may be blessed. amen.

my ex choosing someone else ova me and cutting me off was the best thing that's ever happened to me because then i was alone and then i was forced to love myself and grow and become a better person. like the first two months was hell. i was so upset at the thought of him being with someone else and i would ask him over and over 'what's wrong with me?' i would pick myself apart and compare myself to the girl he chose so many times but looking back i now realize that there was absolutely nothing wrong with me and that i was perfect. it was him that was the problem. i want to call him and thank him tho for turning me into this bad bitch who doesn't need anyone. like deadass. fuck depending on a nigga to validate my self esteem and beauty. i fell back in love with myself and i'm so glad :) it took so

44

many nights of solitude to get to this point in my life. i looked in the mirror this morning and i felt beautiful. i have class later on today and i can't wait to wear something cute and show everyone how cute and amazing i am.

RANDOM SHIT

#TEAMLEMMESEEYODICKPRINTINYOBASKETBALLSHAWTS

*

i love women like 1000 times more than men! women are beautiful, funny, smart, and just honestly 100% better than men! #teamWomen #teamGirls #teamMenAreTrash

i love online shopping so much honestly. i love hunting for things that i want and seeing them on sale or seeing them marked down and i like how it literally takes like 5 seconds to order things and the anticipation of it's arrival is so great like? i've been making an effort to rebuild my wardrobe and get grown and sexy nude tones instead of colorful random shit that doesn't go with anything else i own. like the other day i ordered two dresses from american apparel (in black and nude) and a vintage calvin klein denim jacket. i've been having my eye on this alexander wang cardigan and i want to splurge on essentials that will last me for years and years. i love expensive quality pieces because i feel like they are so versatile! there's so much that i need to get because i'm basically getting rid of all the clothes i have and replacing them with nothing but high quality essentials. i feel like i've outgrown a lot of 'trendy' type shit. i just want to be on my grown and sexy shit for the year 2015 honestly. AND THEN ONCE I GET ALL MY NEUTRAL TONED ESSENTIALS I WILL THEN START INCORPORATING POPS OF COLOR :)

ima huge fan of people that only speak on what they know about.

seeing pretty black girls
uplifting other pretty black girls
makes me so happy.

showering after exercising is the best thing eva! like dead ass!!!!! it's like 'u worked hard hoe! now here's ur reward!!!! u get to clean the sweat off yo body!

if u can make me laugh like really really laugh no fake shit, U SPECIAL! because I'm generally unimpressed and i don't genuinely laugh at a lot of shit. i do that fake lil laugh because i'm a fake bitch.

hair compliments are the best compliments to me because like hair is so important.

i love black women. we so pretty and soft :)

idk about u but i have no problem complimenting a bad bitch when i see one!

is proud of myself for even showing up to class

things that make my pussy wet
going to the bank
getting a check
seeing shit i love on sale in MY size
a full tank of gas
wearing my fav outfit
having a good face, hair and eyebrow day

my favorite thing in this world is putting niggas on to songs they haven't heard before.

sneaks in ur bedroom at night while u sleepin

rubs castor oil on ur edges and eyelashes

rubs coconut oil in ur hair

rubs some cocoa butter on ur elbows

kisses u on the forehead

BROWN/BLACK GIRLS ARE TAKING OVER FOR 2014. I CAN SEE IT.
WE GONE FINALLY GET THE RECOGNITION AND LOVE THAT WE DESERVE.

i used to be totally against crying and i used to almost feel ashamed ana embarrassed and weak for crying but the older and more mature i get, i've become a fan of crying like forreal!!!!! like if u need to cry, cry!!!! ur not weak or corny for crying! it's okay to be #vulnerable. after i cry i have so much clarity and i feel this weird sense of calm wash over me? and i feel less stressed. also! i feel like it's very therapeutic and necessary because ur literally just letting all of ur feelings and emotions out in a way that doesn't harm others or harm urself. it's really great honestly.

this is kind of corny BUT i love late night phone conversations because they feel so sincere? like the person ur talking to is getting vulnerable with u and ur getting vulnerable with them and the person that they are in the day time is the mask they put on for other people to see but when ur talking to them during the night that mask is slowly kind of peeling off and u get to see them for the person that they really are! like all of their negative thoughts, their insecurities, their worries, the shit that bothers them low-key …their dreams. the good…the bad…all of it and it's so overwhelming and exciting that they would let u get a glimpse of the R E A L them.

eyebrow compliments are above all compliments.

no offense but black girls are the prettiest.

i'm a huge fan of bitches that immediately walk out of the bathroom when i enter the bathroom because they respect my right of privacy to take selfies or fix my hair.

that feeling of peace and tranquility that washes over u after u finally deleted all of the unflattering pics of urself.

everytime i see a cute ass black girl on campus i say silently in my head: 'yes sis slay a lil bit'!

um God was really showing out when he made black women like? we look good as hell!

that fresh out the shower feeling is the best feeling on this earth and no other feeling can duplicate it.

planning events around
what ur hair and eyebrows look like.

i'm soooo corny but it makes me feel so good when someone tells me something that they are genuinely excited or happy about. like i feel like i actually matter bc i crossed ur mind and u were so excited and couldn't wait to tell me what made u happy.

it's scientifically proven that if u can make me laugh til i'm in tears, ur chances of digging in these walls are up at like 80.5%

i'm such a grandma. all day i'm like "i can't wait to get up in that bed and go to sleepppppppp chile". bedtime is literally my fav part of the day.

i don't think ya'll understand how important nails are to me.

u know what really makes me happy tho? being at a red light and seeing someone jam out to music in their car and going bananas over whatever banger they are listening to.

my testimony:
baby wipes saved my life.
baby wipes honestly makes shitting a positive experience.
like u don't have to dread that itchy burning sensation in ur ass.
toilet tissue is not enough.
the crack of ur ass deserves more.
U DESERVE MORE.

what if we lived in a world where u could go out without wearing a bra and everyone was mature about it.

i need a nigga i can trust and a nigga that's down for me.

who tryna purchase me a cute ass puppy that will be loyal to me til the end?

those days when u look just as hawt in your selfie as u do in the mirror <3

i love it when a white person apologizes and is suddenly so remorseful after some footage or audio has been leakea of them saying some racist ass shit. like NOOOOOOO CRACKER WHAT U SAID THE FIRST TIME IS WHAT U MEANT. UR JUST STRESSED THAT UR WALLET IS GOING TO BE HURT.

things that get me so emotional:

1. hood niggas

2. a good neptunes instrumental

3. a denim on denim look done successfully

4. baby hair

5. dark skin niggas in polo

currrent mood: suck on my titties and tell me how pretty i am as i'm telling u about how my day went

2003 was a great year and if u have to ask why, i'm judging u bitch!

getting money makes me so wet honestly.

when i get up to heaven ima ask God why these raggedy ass hoes wouldn't let me live while i was on earth and why niggas stay taking pics in front of cars that they do not own tryna floss for the gram!

people who dismiss ur feelings are so annoying like if i tell u I'm feeling some typa way and u hit me wit that 'YEAH U ALRIGHT.' 'U'LL BE AIIGHT' i'm never telling u how i feel again.

Buying expensive, heavy textbooks that you'll never even open in class.

'i'm black and 1/4 irish'
CONGRATS HOE! U STILL BLACK!

being grown as hell and still afraid of ur mama.

why be a liar? it's so gross and unnecessary plus the person ur being dishonest with will find out in the end eventually lmao like pls

I hate when I see people complaining about the job they have, bitch at least you have a job and you ain't struggling to get hired. Shit. if you don't like yo job, give it to me.

if i call u and u reply to me with a text, we throwin hands. square up bc i should be a priority. u better drop every single thing u doing when i call because i don't call ppl often so if i call u first, u betta feel special.

racist ass white people and self hating ass niggas got our black lil babies questioning themselves or doubting whether they are good enough and comparing themselves to their white peers and feeling like they will never measure up and that shit just makes me so fucking upset like??

ppl who over use gay lingo make me uncomfortable.

i'm sick of some of u hoes telling me to humble myself etc etc. i need to fuck with myself and stan for myself since no one else is? like i am not going to turn down my self confidence just so u hoes can feel comfortable! fuck i look like!

young nigga wit a hollister shirt on that's 2 sizes too small, a shell necklace, blue contacts, cargos and flip flops.

what you said: when dark skin girls have blonde hair they look like duracell batteries hahahahahahaha
what i heard: i'm a self hating ass negroid

i am so proud to say i have neva seen or touched a white dick!

the embarassment and the mortification of looking like a broke bitch when ur card is declined.

if u diss any music,fashion or pop culture from the 90's/ early 2000's,
ur a lame ass bitch
and i can never associate w/ u.

i really feel some typa way when i see someone being dragged for having bad skin or acne. like? having bad skin has nothing to do with hygiene or whatever. like before u make fun of someone's skin think about how it would feel to have bad skin. how it would feel to always be self conscious about how ur skin looks under different lighting or not wanting to go out when u have a bad breakout? making fun of someone for their skin is not cool.

all i honestly associate with school is stress, feelings of inadequacy, deadlines, and anxiety.

u gotta be the shittiest person in the whole wide world to abuse an animal or a child.

I HATE WHEN PPL TRY TO GET TOO CLOSE TO ME TOO FAST LIKE PLS THIS IS TOO OVERWHELMING AND STRESSFUL FOR ME.

let me let u white hoes in on a lil secret. just because u may be fucking with a black dude and have black dick inside of u doesn't give u hoes a license to utter the word 'nigga'.

preying on someone's insecurities and making fun of them (even in a joking way) is the most fucked up shit you can do to a person bc they'll forever remember what you said.

people who only wanna talk to u when they need a favor are the worst kind of ppl. fucking leeches.

do some flagrant disrespectful ass slick shit to me
and i will drop u
like an artist
from bad

boy records.

get the fuck away from me if u smoke cigarettes bruh. u not finna give me no second hand lung cancer. noooo thanks. my lungs finna stay pink like my pussy.

yo it hurts like hell when my black friends say shit like 'he's too dark i wouldn't date him. i only like light skin niggas' and i'm just like B I T C H what the hell is wrong with dark skin? like? hoe u dark too? do u not love urself? colorism is still such an issue and it's sad seeing our people not love their own skin tone and i'm just like ???? i understand people got preferences but like??????

i'm mad that we live in a kind of world where a rapper gets praise for featuring a dark skin girl in his music video. it should be normal to have a dark skin girl in a music video.

if you say ginger spice was your fav spice girl i'm judging you.

y is it sooooo shocking that black women can have long hair.

pls get the fuck away from me if you think rape jokes are funny.

what you said: racism no longer exists.
what i heard: i'm a delusional ass bitch who chooses to be blind to what the fuck is goin on.

it irritates me when i see women put down other women for their preferences in hair and makeup. like if a bitch want to wear a 22 inch malaysian sew in with a contoured face and long eyelashes that is her business!!!!! u hoes kill me with that 'she so fake. i bet it takes her forever to get ready in the morning' type bullshit. like look, just because u may not wear much makeup or rock ur real hair, don't put down the next bitch for doing her thang!!!!! growUp.org

some light skin folks love to play a game called 'let's pretend colorism doesn't exist. let's call dark skin people bitter instead.

i hate when parents shame their child about premarital sex. and make them go to these lil purity group thangs and get purity rings. the whole 9 yards. i'm just like??? when i become a mom or whatever ima just let my child know that the world is wild and be s@fe.com about what u do and ur not a bad person if u make the decision to have sex before marriage. it's ur body and ur choice and ultimately ur life. just love urself enough to be S A F E cuz niggas be havin da rabies (stds).

i really want to fucking vomit when i see the bodies of young black girls being sexualized! u old niggas are fucking disgusting! why the fuck would u even look at a child in that way????

dear white people,

if u touch my fucking afro, be prepared to touch these hands.

sincerely, me.

it's so gross when people tell me 'omg u sound like a white girl' and act all shocked and surprised when i speak as if speaking well can only be associated with white people :/

btw you're a wack ass bitch if you have the fact that you're mixed in your description on your blawg or in yo twitter name.

i think it's really sad and gross how black women continue to defend black men but we can't get the same thing reciprocated. some black men are really out here cooning for the white man! like i really can't!!!!!! especially u respectability ashy ankh niggas! u think ur trying to further our race and get us to "DO BETTER" but ur honestly not doing shit but trying to police black women!

i really don't understand why ya'll think cheating and having side hoes or 'fucking someone's man' is cute or something to be proud of. at the end of the day, u playing with people's feelings and that shit is not cool at all. like dead ass. think about how yo ass would feel if someone was running game on u. stop it.

i get so anxious and stressed when i start to think about what ima do with the rest of my life! a bitch ain't ready 2 grow up yet!!!!!!

nothing honestly gets me more livid than a white person saying 'ur racist towards white people'. like naw hoe shut the fuck up. yo white ass ain't allowed to say that shit. call me when ur people are getting killed for just existing. call me when ur women are the punchline to every joke on twitter and instagram. call me when ur culture is being appropriated and sold right the fuck back to u. C A L L M E.

yt ppl who try so hard to be "down" are the most annoying type of yt ppl. just be yourself jesus.

non black poc saying the word 'nigga' makes me just as uncomfortable as when a white person says it!

until u have ur shit together, u can't tell me shit and even if u do have ur shit together u still can't tell me shit because everyone gets their shit together at different times okay.

if u were my friend and u decided to throw away our friendship over some dick,
ur dead to me and i'll never talk to u ever again.
dick comes and go but fly
bitches like me come once in a life time.
pls don't get it twisted.

i feel so embarrassed when someone calls me and i was asleep. i answer the phone like i was all alert and shit. i never wanna be caught slippin, ya feel me?

if u go to college, don't be an ass wipe and put down ppl who don't go to college or try to make them feel like they are less than u.

if i call u and u text me back instead of calling me back, ima find ur location and beat ur ass.

my number one pet peeve in this entire world is when people say they are going to do something and then don't do it. like pls don't flex or stunt on me when we're supposed 2 hang out because bitch i left my home for u. i left the comfort of wifi and air condition for u. i wrote u into my busy (not really busy because ion have 2 much of a life but that's besides the point) schedule and when u flex on me or curve me when u said u wanted to hang out....i consider u 2 be fake and a L I A R and i'm the only one allowed 2 be fake in this world good bye.

white men w/ user names such as 'i love black women' and white men that call us 'chocolate' 'caramel' etc are never to be trusted. we are not some fucking fetish or flavor. like do u want a fucking cookie or a pat on the back because u love women of color? u think u deserve some type of reward for loving us? nah. u just look creepy. stop calling us chocolate, caramel, etc. stop calling us corny shit like 'nubian african goddess'. just stop bruh.

following a nigga and seeing nothing but light skin bitches w/ a 3c curl pattern all over his blawgg that look nothing like u.

i'm so fucking sick of men telling us what we can and cannot wear!!!!! if a bitch wanna rock a neon yellow lip or if baby girl wanna wear red eyeshadow w/ a purple lip who the fuck are u to tell her she can't pull it off!!!!!!!! shut the fuck up. what if i told yo crusty ass yo short ashy dick don't suit ur body or what if i snatched off yo fitted and told u that ur receding hair line didn't fit u!!!!!!!!

if u don't kiss me after i suck u up, it's ova.
bye.

black people who try to police other black people for using the word 'nigga' kill me.

"that little girl was always so fast"

"she knew what she was doing"

that's the reason why victims of sexual abuse don't come forward and keep quiet about what the fuck happened to them because ya'll love to victim blame. don't be a shitty person and blame the victim for what happened to them.

if u negative as fuck and u have this negative outlook on life or u always complaining about shit, then get the fuck from around me because i work hard to stay positive and i put in a lot of effort to fight off any negative thoughts so i don't need another person inserting any negative energy into my life!

a racially ambiguous girl with 3c hair sucking on a lollipop will get like 55555858585858558585 notes but a dark girl with 4c hair will get like 200 notes doing the same shit. ya'll are so fake LOL

if u smoke cigarettes, u'll neva have a chance with me because we can't grow ola together because u gone be dead from cancer.

yoooooo i love makeup but i hate reading the comments on a before and after makeup picture collage because in the comments niggas are so judgmental and

56

basically make women feel like shit for wearing makeup, like we're trying to "decieve" them? they expect every woman to just have flawless skin and eyebrows etc. oh and God forbid we have acne. NEWS FLASH: WE DON'T WEAR MAKEUP FOR YA'LL.

i hate when ppl only dwell on the plastic surgery that lil kim has had done. let's talk about her talent and the various iconic looks mama has given us. Let's talk about THAT.

LOL black men slander black women like every second of the day but get so heated when we start dealing with other races or we stop defending them!!!!!!!!

if you don't use baby wipes to wipe your ass, you're nasty bc tissue does nothing but smear the shit around.

the next time someone asks me how school is going and shit like that, i'm going to drop to the ground and start kicking and crying uncontrollably.

things that give me anxiety:
dirty fingernails
thin barely there eyebrows
shitting without baby wipes
yt ppl w/ dreadlocks

the only reason I want to be at the dentist is to get a grill or to get my teeth bleached. other than that, nawwww bruh

lemme know if ur more outraged at the burning of the american flag than the black lives that have been lost in this country so i can hit ya wit that unfollow real quick.

let's play a game called 'how many white people gone catch these hands if i see them in any black face today?'

if u in a relationship or married pls don't spit game at me or even look my way honestly!!!!!! u ain't gone get me caught up in ya drama!!!!! i am not the one! i'm too cute to be ya side hoe.

i'll never understand the appeal of wanting to fuck someone else's man?? like IDGI.

i have no issue w/ mixed ppl.
my thing is....
some of ya'll love to scream 'i'm mixed' from every single mountain top
and it comes off a lil like 'I'M NOT FULLY BLACK. YASSSSSSSS.'

if i'm dealing with a nigga and i'm feeling him or whatever.... a huge deal breaker for me would be hearing him talk shit about other black women. like i don't care how cute u are or how great u suck my titties or how great ur stroke game is. dissing black women is like dissing my mother, my sisters etc. A L S O if u dissing us and ur a black man it's clearly evident to me that u don't love urself so how can u ever learn to love M E ? ? ?

i can't stand a 'lemme get out the sun so i won't get darker' ass hoe.

i'm very vain and i'm usually in a bad mood bc of these reasons:
bad hair days
when i can't find shit to wear
when my eyebrows aren't neatly groomed
when my skin breaks out

ur trash in my eyes if u bring a child into this world ana don't make any attempts to take care of it in any type of way.

um if ur on the fence about ferguson or ur on this 'we are the world. we all bleed red. not all white people are bad. let there be world peace. this is beyond race' bullshit unfollow me rn i'm not even fucking kidding. black people are out here dying. this shit ain't a game.

if i hear 'black people got to do better' one more got damn time! it's not us that 'got to do better' it's these damn racist crackers that need to do better like please!!!!!!

*i can't stand "i only like women who wear heels" type niggas. who the fuck cares what u like?? *stomps on ur head with my timbs** *no matter how late i'm running to class or if i overslept, i would NEVER EVER show up to class wearing some fucking pajamas. hoes that do that have no typa home training. i would rather walk into class late looking cute than walking in on time looking like a sack of shit.*

ur a shitty person if u ever made fun of someone that has acne.

um i'm all about supporting people's dreams and what not but some of u niggas need to stop rapping! like let that shit go because it ain't it for u!!!!! stop flexing on the innanet like u out here making coins when ur really not! stop posting pics of luxury cars and stacks of money that ain't even urs! stop sending everyone and their mama a link to ur mixtape! u niggas are like the jehovah fucking witness bitches wit that shit!!!!! stop the corniness!!!

i be sitting in the financial aid office like drake sitting in that chair.

the fact that u can simply dye ur hair pink, blue, or purple and u won't be called a ghetto ass hood rat bitch. the fact that u can state ur opinions with out being labeled 'angry' or 'feisty' because ur white. the fact that niggas on twitter don't go in on how nappy ur hair is, how dark ur skin is, or how ur a bald bitch because LOL black girls can't grow hair. the fact that ur people aren't being fucking slaughtered for just existing. the fact that people don't assume u are angry on a fucking website because LOL u haven't met ur father or ur father isn't in ur life. or how about the fact that boys on the school bus are laughing at ur hair because it resembles 'pubic hair' to them? or the fact that u can walk into literally any store and see images of bitches that look like ur white ass everywhere. ur plastered all over the billboards. magazines. television. white bitches are STILL the standard of beauty and i'm fucking sick of it. i'm fucking angry and i have every fucking right to be angry about it. so don't fucking sit here and tell me i have no right to be angry about this shit. until u experience the shit i've experienced as a black woman ur white ass don't have the right to say shit.

hair is such a senstive ass topic for me omg. i get sooooo much shit from "friends", family members, strangers, and niggas about my hair. like "why you cut it?" "i wonder what you look like w/ a straight long weave" "you should wear a weave" "when you getting your hair done" "what you doing to your hair next" and like even in high school when i had a perm or whatever, i used to wear my hair curly and i would get teased and niggas would say my hair was nappy etc. and i used to literally come home from school crying bc i was constantly ridiculed about my hair. even now, i still get comments on my hair. i'm sry all these comments about Beyoncé's hair is such a trigger for me. it's a damn shame that ppl are soooo hung up about some hair. the next person that makes a comment about my hair ima tell them to munch on my ass. i don't owe a single explanation to no fucking body about the way i wear my hair. this shit is getting ridiculous!!!

shit that's hard
being an adult
keeping fresh fruit around

why is it that dark skin women are called 'bitter' or 'insecure' when we get angry about not being represented enough in the media? what is so wrong about wanting to see more of urself on the runway, magazines, tv, etc? what is so W R O N G??????????????????

me complimenting someone: *BITCCCHHH BItchHH B I T C H!!!! CAN U FUCKING let me live my life?! TURN ON UR LOCATION SO U CAN CATCH THESE HANDS FOR LOOKING SO FUCKING GOOD! what In The Hell?! LIKE PLEASE!!!!*

people who try to tear u down and make u feel bad about urself under the guise of humor/jokes are the worst type of people.

tacky ass ppl do shit like compare aaliyah and Beyoncé, and rock micheal kors/coach bags.

POP CULTURE

THE BABY PINK VELOUR TRACKSUIT, THE GOLD HOOP EARRINGS,
AND THE BABY HAIR J.LO WAS ROCKING IN THE I'M REAL REMIX
VIDEO WAS ICONIC.

*

Beyoncé always inspires me to level the fuck up!

when i see black folks dragging baby blue ivy about her hair and why it's 'not done' or 'not combed' all i see is 'I HATE MYSELF. I HATE MY BLACKNESS.'

every time i listen to André 3000 also known as 3 stacks also known as André Lauren Benjamin, i am grateful that i even have ears and i feel blessed that they work properly.

i love the movie 'crooklyn' so much because it's so random like life is? and it beautifully displays that the most fucked up shit can happen to ordinary people to help them grow?

shoutout to the nigga that came up with the brilliant idea to have violin strings play in the background of sisqo's 'thong song' !!!!!

i'll never get over Beyoncé being a sneaky ass bitch and releasing all that shit on us in the middle of the night like that.

*jennifer lopez gave us glam
in the form of a velour tracksuit!
GIVE HER SOME DAMN RESPECT.*

i'll never get over how gorgeous lupita nyong'o is so pls don't ask me to. thanks.

lil b's tweets are so positive and cute. i wanna fuck him.

willow smith is so pretty and so confident and so sure of herself! she's comfortable in her skin when most girls her age have the most self doubt! i wish i was as comfortable with myself at that age! i envy willow! i really do!

bitch! in 2005, chris brown was my light skint boyfriend! couldn't nobody tell me he wasn't talking to me on that cd!!!!!!!!

has anybody ever noticed that aaliyah's hair was always laid to perfection? like she didn't have a single bad hair day. 1 have never seen one picture of her hair looking jank. not one.

meagan good's cups runneth over praise gawd

mya's blue jersey dress in the best of me part 2 video is a very important look 2 me.

WWMD = What. Would. Moesha. Do.

if u stan for eminem or iggy azalea ur trash in my eyes.

current emotion:
hurricane chris's hair beads

i think about Beyoncé's makeup look in the music video for the song Jealous.mp3 a lot and it makes me so emotional because she looks so vulnerable and beautiful and if this look doesn't scream fall/winter then i don't know what does? like?

chris brown is that type of nigga that u still wanna fuck even tho u know he ain't no good for u. like all he gotta do is grab u by the waist a lil bit and kiss on yo neck and u forget all the jank shit he's done temporarily. then later on u in the bed crying because ur mad at urself for still fucking w/ this no good ass nigga.

remember in 2001 when Beyoncé was a hawt ass rapper in "Carmen: A Hip Hopera?"

Jennifer Hudson gets on my fucking nerves.

halle berry's best role is "b.a.p.s" and she should have won an oscar for that, not for fucking billy bob thorton's crusty yt ass.

when i was younger and i used to watch ashanti's videos (or any r&b music video basically).

every time they showed a bitch packing shit in her louis vuitton bag

they literally always showed her dropping her luggage at the end of the music video and taking that trifilin' nigga back.

i used to think to myself, wtf y she taking this nigga back?!

now i'm older and i understand it can be hard to stawp dealing w/ a no good ass nigga right away. sometimes u convince urself that the nigga will change and do better. sometimes ur young and stupid and u don't love urself enough to know when enough is enough.

james franco look like he then been thru some thangs and not in a good typa way. smh.

solange's wedding was really ethereal and beautiful and everyone looked like they descended from heaven and i love the fact that she had the wedding in new orleans because i'm from new orleans btw and that makes me so happy and i love that lil video of her and julez dancing to 'no flex zone' and i'm still salty as hell that i didn't get an invitation. and i really love how ms tina has truly glo'd up! like she looked so snatched and she out here killing the young hoes and serving the children. like she is a prime example that upgrading and getting new dick can change u for the better honestly. and bitch did u see Beyoncé shape in that fucking dress like she is bad as hell and i was like O_o at her hips! and i was living for solange's cape and afro like BBITCHHHHH. i handed her my wig after seeing the pics honestly because i mean like…???? i want to get married but i doubt ima get married any time soon because niggas don't even want to take a bitch out to eat let alone propose lmao. boys are such knuckleheads. i think ima wife myself up. ima rent a place and wear a white versace gown and just dance wit myself because these niggas are knuckleheads.

if u stan for the kardashian/jenner crew then feel free to unfollow me! i don't support racist white hoes that fetisize black men! God bless!

instead of shaming rihanna for that see thru joint she wore at the CFDA fashion awards…. worry about why ur wifi is cut awf rn. worry about why u have to draw ur hairline in wit a damn sharpie. worry about why u faking out here tryna impress niggas who don't give a shit about u. worry about why yo raggedy ass car broke down last week and u had to call a bitch to come take yo ass to work.

worry about why ur bedroom smells like cologne and ass. worry about that damn hot ass breath u have. worry about those shit stains in yo boxers. worry about why u have to jerk off every night to pornhub because u can't get a bitch to fuck ur lame ass. worry about all of that and when ur done u still can't say shit about what rihanna wore. why? because i am here for a black woman wearing whatever the fuck she wants.

in 2009 i was crying to "houstatlantavegas" in my bedroom.

Helga G Pataki is such an inspiration to me because as thirsty as she was for arnold and as much as she wanted to fuck him, she successfully concealed her thirst.

Beyoncé taught me how to love/depend on myself emotionally in "me myself and i"
Beyoncé taught me to pull out that special dress when my nigga ain't acting right in "freakum dress"
Beyoncé taught me that's there's other niggas that's better than a lying cheating ass nigga in "irreplaceable"
Beyoncé taught me how to say the astrological signs in order by month in "signs"
Beyoncé taught me the importance of consent and saying "no" in "yes"
Beyoncé taught me how to channel my inner "sasha fierce" in "diva"
Beyoncé taught me the importance of leaving a legacy in this world in "i was here"
Beyoncé taught me to stawp giving niggas the pussy when they're neglecting u emotionally and physically in "kitty kat"
there's so many important lessons to learn from Beyoncé.

an artist's first era is usually the best bc they have shit to prove. They have to show ppl that they are worth stanning for.

kelis has done everything before ur fav even thought about doing it. let's not get it twisted.

remember in 2005 when everyone thought chris brown said 'my AIDS ain't gonna slow us down' instead of 'my age ain't gonna slow us down' in the hit single 'run it'? LIKE PLEASE.

a list of white women i cared about
teena marie
brittany murphy

the silky pajamas tlc wore in the 'creep' music video is the only acceptable and ideal bedtime look.

knocks on ur window at 5:50 a.m.
SO WHAT PART OF THE FLAWLESS REMIX IS UR FAV PART?

Rihanna's pussy must be golden. I want my pussy to have niggas fighting in the club.

bitch i just saw a recent pic of ashanti and ja rule in the studio. omg they finna take us back to 2001. GURLLL YO STARE...THOSE EYYYEEE— EEEEE-IIIIII—-SSSS LOVE IT WHEN U LOOK AT ME BAAAAAAAYYYY BEHHHH.

omarion's choreography in the 'touch' video was amazing and ur a raggedy cunt bag if u don't think so.

Beyoncé is so fucking thick and even more bootylicious than she was before. I bet jay digging in her vaginal walls with a spoon and eating it like ice cream.

i still remember the day i found out aaliyah died. it was a sunday (like today) and it was right before church (when i used to go) and my momma told me and i was in disbelief. like that shit caught me soooo off guard. rest in peace ma. you were beautiful on the inside and out.

I never understood what the fuck sean paul was saying but he made good pussy poppin music and that was good enough for me.

yrs later and i'm still in shock that mariah carey married and had children with nick cannon. i'll never get over it.

i love how aaliyah was singing about a nigga's good stroke game in 'rock the boat'!

i will always love lil kim because she taught me to never let a nigga fuck if he won't eat my pussy.

loooolll I loved how the gross sisters from the proud family was all about their fucking paper like real ass bitches!!!!!

Rozanda 'Chilli' Thomas = the baby hair queen

ur not a stan if u only list singles as ur fav songs by an artist.

Beyoncé got that "u can tell that ass phat even from the front" typa body.

when i find myself in a dilemma or a sticky situation,
i think to myself
'what would moesha do?'

if ur a celeb and u look a mess, fucking right i'm dragging ur ass. u have absolutely no excuse. u have access to the best hair care, skin care, dental care, and fashion.

Beyoncé's "yes" is my fav 'nigga i ain't fucking u' song.

all maaaa life i been feeling like effie in the movie dream girls but bitch in 2014 ima be deena. 2014 is maaaa yearrr.

the zillion dollar girls taught ya'll hoes that aero ain't nothing. pls never forget that.

I wonder what Beyonce's sex life with Jay is like. Does Jay eat pussy? Does Beyonce suck Jay's dick?....Have they done 69? Is Beyonce a noise-maker? I bet Jigga be demolishing Bee's pussy walls.

Andre 3000's "The love Below" changed my life.

if u like katy perry please don't follow me!!!! thanks!!!!

btw, if ur a black man and ur rushing to iggy's defense but haven't said a word about the black women that are relentlessly getting ridiculed and bashed everyday, u are a coon. end of story. bye.

current emotion: Beyoncé's ponytail in 'upgrade u'

imagine if amber rose and blac chyna got together and wrote a new york times best selling book about the shit they have endured being married to men in the industry accompanied with a vh1 reality tv show. LIKE BITCH!!!!

r.kelly literally is that 47 yr old uncle that u see at the family reunion that's still rocking a fitted, baggy jeans, and timbs. no one has the heart to tell his old ass to dress his actual age.

ya'll manny from degrassi was like my favorite character low-key. She did some hoe shit every episode and my black ass was here for it.

i really fucking believe ya'll say "i like kelly rowland better" just because u can't find a justifiable reason not to like Beyoncé!

i wish amber rose was my baby mama.

if u don't find lupita nyong'o attractive u blind bruh.

as much as I shade rihanna, I low-key be checking for her in some type of way.

can we pls take a moment out of our day to talk about how nicole murphy's body is shitting on everything?

i can't fucking stana draya! bitches that don't take care of their kids will never get any sympathy from me! don't be a shitty mother and put material possessions and dick before ur kids.

I love Beyoncé but I will never be caught dead in house of dereon. I ride for Beyoncé but I can't waste my money on some shit that's falling apart AND I don't even see her wearing it except in the ads. LMAO.

Lupita Nyong'o makes me so proud to be a black woman. not only did she slay her role in 12 years a slave but she can dress her ass off and she just has this inner radiance about her that is so infectious and undeniable. she is so important to me. i want to see more of her and i want to see her succeed. she is someone all the little black babies can look up to! i deadass thought she was gonna get slept on and not win but she did and i'm so proud of her! she is shitting on everyone so effortlessly!

i think it's really gross how niggas are already saying that amber rose is going to take all of wiz's money or that she was the one that cheated just because she used to be a stripper. *takes a sip of green tea* goes to show u how 90% of the time men are not held responsible for their actions. somehow it's always the woman's fault.

i'm soooo mad that ya'll still stanning for a$ap rocky after he made that lipstick comment.

pls search for ur edges before u come for little blue ivy's hair.
bitch ur grown and ur coming for a fucking baby because of her hair?
some of ya'll are fucking ridiculous.
meanwhile blue ivy chilling in italy while yo broke bitter pathetic ass using mcdonald's wifi (bc u don't have it at home) to drag blue ivy for her hair.
worry about where ur edges are. worry about why u only have 5 strands of hair in ur fucking head bc ur priorities are clearly in the wrong order.

Raven Symoné is a delusional ass hoe and to think that i used to stan for this bitch. i am so upset. like? all the new black hoes are coming out the closet this year i swea.

if u like miley cyrus or support any of her appropriating bullshit, unfollow me rn.

When Chris Brown first came out, that nigga was the epitome of what a light skin nigga was supposed to be. Those juicy lips, that peanut shaped head, those dark beady eyes, those veins popping out of the side of his head when he sang certain shit. The typical oversized t-shirts, baggy jeans, and sneakers. That lisp. he gave me everything I needed. lawd. the memories.

I wish more thought and creative concepts were put into music videos like how it was back in the day.

remember the episode when manny decided to be a hoe? i was so annoyed w/ emma because emma wouldn't support her decision to be a hoe! like what type of best friend are u bitch? tryna police manny's sexuality! GIRL BYE!

drake been laying the pipe so good that rihanna has barely been tweeting or posting on instagram in the last 3 weeks. lmaooooo

celebrities that have made themselves look dumb as hell regarding the situation in ferguson

1. draya michele

2. sza

3. keke palmer

4. jhene aiko

if i would be a song, i would be 'no angel' because i'm a serious slept on banger! everyone loves 'partition' but only a few check for 'no angel' and that is officially me. under appreciated.

yells at u in a mystikal tone of VOICE

lupita nyong'o has been giving us amazing looks consistently non stop and if u ain't talking about that shit then what the fuck u talking bout hoe?

everytime i listen to tamia's 'so into you' i feel like dropping out of school and starting a family and walking along the beach while the sun sets holding my baby girl on my hip and dusting the sand off her lil baby feet.

"me myself and i" is probably my fav Beyoncé song because it encourages u to be ur own source of happiness ana that is the most important thing in this life.

my fav part of bring it on is when the east compton clovers call out the yt girls and get them the fuck together for stealing their cheers <3 tryna steal our bit but you look like shit but we're the ones who were down with it.

tupac = ideal boyfriend type

i was gonna skip class today then i thought of lupita and i decided to get my black ass up and go to class.

remember when stomp the yard came out and chris brown died before u could even go put some more butter on ur popcorn?

when i was younger, i remember watching tlc's video for 'waterfalls' and being scared to even have sex. lmao.

reasons why r.kelly still has a career
no one gives a shit about black women

i'm manny santos, ur emma nelson.

Beyoncé
make
me
wanna
do
better.

GOALS

I JUST WANNA BE FINANCIALLY STABLE WHILE DOING SOMETHING I REALLY FUCKING LOVE AND I WANT HEALTHY RELATIONSHIPS THAT HELP ME EVOLVE INTO AN EVEN BETTER PERSON THAN I ALREADY AM!

*

i want to be so financially secure that i don't even think to glance at the price tag of anything.

i pray everyday that when i hit my 40's, ima look like Nia long.

when i become a mom, i will never force my child to go to church!

yo like dead ass i'm tryna be in my nike gear from head to toe at all times so i can start sprinting or running in place at any given moment. i'm tryna be one of those ppl that wake up before the sun comes up to run. i am tryna be fitness mami. no process foods mami. what's a carb? what's candy?

reasons i want to throw a party
to wear a cute ass look and shit on everyone there
to make a hawt ass playlist

bitch what If someone found a cure for acne and it was in pill form and u only had to take that one pill and u would never have a breakout ever again for the rest of ur life.

me as a mom: *pulls up in my ice blue mercedes truck blasting soulja slim to pick up the lil babies from ballet practice*

it's time for me to grow the hell up and get a leather black bag and my titties pierced!!!!

like dead ass, i'm tryna have niggas sprung. i want niggas to feel some typa way when i don't call them back. i want niggas to look over at my face to detect any

72

signs of approval from me when we watching a movie he picked. i want niggas to be simping HARD. i'm tryna have niggas deleting instagram accounts and twitter accounts without hesitation. i want niggas to be scared to speak of another bitch in my presence.

dials 911

911: *what's ur emergency?*

me: *i need some d*ck from a nigga that's about shit!*

I just want to sell every single piece of clothing I have and start all over and get a whole new wardrobe.

i want my future daughter to be so confident and comfortable with herself that when a nigga compliments her she be like 'i know'. i just want to tell her she's beautiful and amazing every single day that she gets sick of hearing it <3 <3 <3

man when i have kids i'm going to immerse them in 90's/early 2000's culture so much. i'm finna tell them about every ja rule and ashanti collab, they finna know about the importance of fubu, rocawear, babyphat etc. i'm going to be that embarassing mom that's blasting ja rule in the mini van when i pick them up from school. i can't wait. oh and when they have friends ova for a sleep over, ima make them all watch "set it off" and "moesha".

if i was filthy rich…… i would wear hawt ass expensive shit all the time for no fucking reason at all. got an errand to run at walmart. aiight *slips on versace dress*

ideal relationship:

I HATE CHUUUU JOOOEEEEDEFEEEEEL!

when i become a mom, i'm going to be strict about leaving my children alone w/ ppl because sexual abuse is r e a l out here. like once ur child is abused, it's too late. the damage has been done. ur child will have emotional scars for the rest of their life. i'm sorry but i rather be seen as 'the mean ass mom' than let my child go thru some traumatic shit like that.

i'm tryna have clear urine for the rest of my life. i want it to look like i didn't even pee, u feel me?

when i have a little girl, i'm going to punish her if i see her bring a yt doll into my home and if she don't have any black friends, ima ground her.

ideal relationship : being so comfortable around a nigga that you shit w/ the door open, fart, burp, wear no makeup, hair all fucked up, gain weight and he still thinks ur the baddest <3

reasons i want to be filthy ass rich
hair stylist
makeup artist
personal trainer

um if i had my own apartment, i would never go to class and i would just bounce on dick all day and watch movies and eat ice cream.

my future:
living in a nice spacious loft with neutral colored walls and black furniture
wearing alexander wang and carrying celine/Balenciaga bags
with a baby girl and a husband that i love

I just want to drop out of college and play with barbies for the rest of my life.

I wish I was a 90's r&b singer that wore tommy Hilfiger boxers and sucked on a lollipop.

me as a mom: get that yt doll out of my home

i'm forcing myself to go to the gym today because bitch ion want no waist. i want to be waistless. all i want is ass and titties and some thick thighs. i want niggas to be asking where my waist at.

me as a mom: *did u eat the mango i packed in ur lunch bag baby?*

i lowkey had this idea of creating a magazine for young women of color. growing up, i stayed reading teen vogue and seventeen. Seldomly did they have a black girl on the cover or discussed topics related specifically related to us. i'm changing my major from art to journalism since i love writing so much. the magazine would contain fashion, young black women that are in the media (television, music, movies etc.), issues that are important specifically to us etc. etc. The magazine would also encourage good self esteem, positivity, and most importantly self love. fitness, relationships, and other things would be discussed every issue.

me after my husband says his vows at our wedding: wow i'm loving this concept.

yall i just wanna ride off into the sunset in a convertible mercedes benz w/ janet jackson's 'somebody to call my lover' playing and i'm sucking on a lollipop wearing cut off denim shorts and smiling and laughing bc i have no responsibilities in life bc i'm filthy rich and young.

i will never be that mother that comes home from work and bitches/nags at my kids about what needs to be done.

things i want for christmas
healthy long hair
a complexion that glows
a hood nigga
Beyoncé to finally give me the full version of something
a huge cute ass water bottle that carries a lot of water so i can stay hydrated
a life time supply of baby wipes
a personal trainer
a makeup artist
a life time supply of gum
black lingerie

i need more money!!!!!!!!!!!! i wanna scream!!!!!! like how do i find an old white nigga that will buy me bape and pay all my bills!!!!!

goals i'm working towards
a 24 inch waist and a fat ass
a nice cozy lil apartment
a better paying job!
my instagram modeling career!

when i become a mom, i'm not gonna talk shit about my child on the phone w/ other family members, i'll only say positive things about my child :)

i want to write a book! like dead ass! i wanna write a fictional juicy urban drama that's scandalous as fuck! but i'm not sure what the subject matter would be exactly. it could possibly be like sex and the city but for black women??? but idk?

me at my wedding: security get this bitch outta here! she looked at my husband for 5 seconds 2 long!!!! this hoe think she me!!!!

u know what i think about a lot?
what i would look like
w/ a lot money,
a stylist,
a makeup/hair team,
and a personal trainer.

me as a grandma: U DON'T KNO NOTHIN ABOUT THAT TEENA MARIE BABY!

um *turns on mic* when i have a dorter, i'm going to compliment her every single day and i'm going to constantly reinforce in her head all the positive things about herself and i'm going to make her fall in love with herself and if any fuck boy makes her cry then he betta be prepared to square up ana duke it out wit her mama (aka me)!!!!

i'm honestly just tryna level up spiritually, mentally, financially, physically, and emotionally!!!!

my wedding vows:
finally.
a
nigga
that's about shit.

how am i going to start a family if i keep running from dick??

my prayer for 2014:

pls God make my hair longer and stronger

my complexion glow

my body healthy and

my ass fatter

amen.

when i have kids, i am not going to tell them fantasy bullshit stories like santa claus coming down the chimney and bringing gifts. i want em to know the truth. i'm not about to give a fat old yt man all the credit. fuck that. ima keep it 100% like I PURCHASED THESE GIFTS 4 U BABY.

Some of the bops i want played at my wedding reception
Soulja Boy feat. Mario - Soulja Girl
Jagged Edge feat. Nelly - Where The Party At
Ca$h Out - Cashin' Out
Tamia - So Into You
Juvenile - Rodeo
Koffee Brown - After Party
Beyoncé - In Da Club (Remix)
Cherish - Do it to it
Fantasia - When i See You
Teena Marie featuring Birdman - Off The Chain
jennifer lopez - i'm real
Ghost Town DJ's - My Boo
Lil Jon & The East Side Boyz featuring Usher & Ludacris - Lovers and friends
Andre 3000 - Pretty Pink Baby Blue
Da Entourage - Bunny Hop
Teena Marie - You Make Love Like Springtime
Andre 3000 feat. Kelis - Dracula's Wedding
Prince - I Would Die 4 U
Chris Brown - Poppin
Nicole Wray - He Must Know
Andre 3000 - Spread
Tweet featuring Missy Elliott - Turn da Lights Off

Latrelle - House Party
Cam'ron - Hey Ma
Kelis - Sugar Honey Ice Tea
Kelis feat. Andre 3000 - Millionaire
Beyoncé- Signs
Slum Village - Selfish
Cheri Dennis - I Luv U
Ciara - Promise
Ciara - Body Party
Lykke li & Drake - A little Bit (remix)
Lil Flip feat. Lea - Sunshine
Jennifer Lopez - I'm Glad
Kelela - Bank Head
Lil Boosie - Wipe Me Down
Lloyd - Get it Shawty
Mariah Carey - Joy Ride
Mariah Carey feat. Mystikal - Don't Stop (Funkin' 4 Jamaica)
Sade - By Your Side
Sammie feat. Sean Paul - You Should Be My Girl
Spice Girls - Holler
Tink- Bonnie and Clyde

bitch when i get my sew in
i'm going to seek out a nigga that has a motorcycle
so he can ride me around the city and i can channel aaliyah's
look in 'more than a woman'.

u know that part in 'baby boy' when yvette is talking to her homegirl on the phone telling her all about the issues she's having w/ jody…meanwhile, her homegirl's nigga is yelling in the background for her to get off the phone so he can fuck her. then yvette hear her friend moaning saying 'oOOoo i feel uuu girllll'? i think about that part of the movie a lot and i want a relationship like that.

i just want to be a better person!!! i don't want to feel bitter about anything or whatever. i just want to learn from my failures and grow. i want someone to love me for the person that i am and not just what i have to offer them. i want to find happiness in the little things. the fact that my oatmeal turned out perfect this morning. the fact that i'm still alive and breathing. the fact that i'm able to type this shit at this very moment. the fact that i can change my life at any given moment with a small simple action. i also want to think more positively and be more grateful! i want to be able to express my feelings fully and unapologetically! to say 'no' without feeling guilty or embarrassed. i don't want to say 'idk' anymore knowing i really mean 'no'. i just want to be able to say 'no' right away. i just want to be the B E S T version of me i can be.

i'm gonna be a cute sporty glam mom that's obsessed w/ late 90's/ early 2000's pop culture and fashion. i'm going to have a little baby girl w/ afro puffs and i'm going to search on the internet to find her some tommy hilfiger over alls and i'm going to tell her she's cute and beautiful every single day of her life. and i'm going to to cut the balls off of any nigga that makes her doubt her beauty for even one second.

me as a mom: 'DON'T LEAVE THIS HOUSE WITHOUT UR WATER BOTTLE BABYGIRL!'

play some new orleans bounce music at my funeral
don't mourn me. celebrate the hawt bitch i was.

my ideal wedding reception: nothing but new orleans bounce music will be played. me and my husband hit the dancefloor and i change out of my classy vera wang gown into a short sexy versace dress and grind on my husband's dick. pizza hut will cater. there's a separate dance floor for the babies and children. anyone that's trying to upstage me will be thown out immediately by security. all eyes on me, best night of maaa life. no bitch will look hawter than me etc etc etc.

drops out of college to become an instagram model

i want to keep niggas and bitches asking 'WHO IS SHE?'

possible names for my future dawta:
1. kelela 2. troy 3. Halima

my constant thoughts consist of
i need to make more money
i need to level up
i need to stunt on niggas

i can't wait to sway my hips to 'body party' at the family bbq joint and tell my grand chilrunnnn that they don't know nothin bout that old lil bop!

God pls send a nigga in my life that i can trust and believe. a nigga with no instagram or twitter or tumblr. a nigga that's not corny or fake. a nigga i ain't gotta worry about talking to otha hoes. a nigga that knows how amazing i am. i need a nigga that's woke pls God.

i've always wanted to suck a nigga up while he driving and make him swerve on the road and make him hit a coupla cars and crash and shit.

when i become an instagram model, ima remember all the hoes who didn't pay attention to me then ima be like 'nawww don't show me love now that everybody else is'!! 'nawwwww u wasn't fucking w/ me when i didn't have weave in! don't fuck with me now that i got a sew in!!!'

i would suck like 5000 dicks to have perf skin and perf hair.

Beyoncé's body is the definition of slim thick and that's my ultimate body goal!!!!!

i can't wait to teach my little girl to only wash her vagina with water and not soap because the vagina is already self-cleansing and i can't wait to put shea butter on her hair/ aloe vera juice on her face and i can't wait to put her in timbs and afro puffs. my whole family about to have matching outfits!!!!!! so when u see us, u'll already know what's good! catch me picking out fresh fruit with my baby girl on my hip! and my husband holding my Chloé handbag and my Fendi diaper bag stocked with nutritious snacks for our family picnic!!!!

dresses my little baby boy in bape
dresses my little baby girl in polo
decorates my family home like tommy's home in the movie 'belly'
drives an ice blue mercedes truck as the family vehicle

packs organic snacks in my designer lunch bag for me and my babies

thinks positive thoughts all the time

makes love to my successful and sexy husband every night

drinks a glass of white wine every night before bed

reads my babies a bedtime story

is beautiful

is successful

is financially stable

is happy

LIFE OF A BLOGGER (& OTHER TECHNOLOGY)

LOOKS AT A MILLION TUTORIALS ON YOUTUBE DAILY
NEVER DOES THEM

*

it's so wild to me that black girls constantly have to fight for everything even a fucking text post on tumblr dot com that's positive about us? we have to share everything. it has to be ALL girls. when white people say 'all girls' they really just mean white girls loooool.

Text Messages That I hate and Will not respond to:
"lol"
"Baby can you send me a picture?"
"Hey ma"
"k"
"Ok"
"Can we hang out?"
"lmao"
"haha"
"Do you love me?"
"hey stranger"
"why ain't you texting me back?"

lol i despise the ppl on tumblr who have to turn everything into a fucking debate.

i believe there is a special place in hell for ppl that reblog posts and put their url as the caption trying to promote their shitty ass blog.

you know what hurts? finding an iconic amazing pic but it's not in hq.

i'm not getting back on Facebook until i have a sexy husband, a social life, and a baby to show off.

I be getting all types of emotional when I find a rare picture of my fav in HIGH resolution. Like you don't know the joy I get. Like shit like that makes my life worth living. #LifeofABlogger my blog is better than yours.org

I hate bloggers who try too hard to have an offensive or shocking url.

it's so fun leaving ppl mystified about ur sexuality on here and they are in ur ask box so thirsty to find out whether ur straight, bi, gay or whatever.

just bc someone doesn't have a selfie of themselves as their icon pic or post selfies of themselves every day doesn't mean they are insecure about their looks or unattractive. can we pls get that straight.

ya'll say ya'll love me but the lie detector test determined that was a lie because when my selfie was on the dash ya'll hoes acted like ya'll was blind.

if u see a positive text post.... leave it alone? like???? ur negative input is not needed like???

can the science side of tumblr explain to me why am i too good for 90% of the people i come in contact with?

looks at a million tutorials on youtube daily
never does them

i'm so annoyed with the low self esteem posts on tumblr. ya'll be reblogging and posting shit like "i'm such a shitty person"...."i'm not attractive". Like shut the fuck up.

if i don't update anymore, i'm either dead, outgrown this shit, or i'm too distracted by money or dick.

i'm too cute for my phone to be this dry? like?

i only wanna Skype or FaceTime when i look good!
if i ask u to Skype or FaceTime me, i just want u to see me and how good i look.

thinking bout becoming #TeamHousePhone bc my fucking cell is so got damn dry.

u a hoe if u follow me.

i never watermark my shit bc aesthetically it's ugly as hell to see some damn text on a pic or gif, and it's not going to stawp muthafuckas from stealing yo shit. thieves will jack yo shit and not even bother to crop the watermark out. lmao. the audacity and boldness.

if i send u a selfie, u better act like it's the best thing u eva laid eyes on. i better get a reply back in the form of an essay as to why u like it and what not. if u act non chalant about me sending u a pic, i'll never send u a pic of myself again.

i get it. tumblr is a public website. there's a reblog button. but if someone makes a personal post ana tells u not to reblog it and u still do anyway ur trash honestly idc idc.

um to all my white followers, don't be the annoying ass white person to insert urself on a post made specifically ana exclusively for black people. don't invade the little space we carved out for ourselves. don't do that.

i cannot wait until i get some good quality dick so i can log off forever and stop being a fucking geek bitch.

I like to go on "un-following sprees" when I'm on my menstrual cycle.

like it's really sad that black girls have to be reminded that they are worthy of being valued or even attractive. like we have to have tumblrs called 'darkskingirls' or 'blackgirlsarepretty2' to remind us of how amazing we are etc. i love those kind of blogs but it's really fucked up that we have to have them because society has shitted on us so much.

everything is "iconic" to ya'll lol stfu.

i be laughing so hard when ppl make a post saying they are going on a hiatus or deleting. hoe u ain't going no whea! u addicted to this shit bitch! if u delete, yo ass will be right back.

those instagram memes that are pitiful attempts to shame black women or make a mockery of black women are created by ashy niggas who haven't washed their balls in weeks.

if u think that a blog that is a safe space for black women translates into a 'white women hating blog' then u honestly need to grow up! just because we uplift one another as black women doesn't mean we hate white women or we are attacking white women! black women need to honestly stan for themselves because no one else is? the last time i checked u self hating ass niggas wasn't but i'm sleep!!!!

all of the girls i follow are so pretty and kind and i hope they get everything they want outta life.

i want a nigga without a social networking site tbh. like what the fuck are u commenting on other bitch's pics for? why u on instagram drooling on ur keyboard for other bitches? why are there bitches on ur blog that look nothing like me?

i can't wait til all of tumblr gets over amanda bynes.

drinking game ideas: take a shot for every light skin bitch w/ curly hair i see on tumblr

i'd be damned if i'm posting pics of me and u on my social network and u ain't got none of us on urs. nawww! i'm not looking like no desparate ass bitch. BYE.

u lean in to kiss my luscious full lips
stops u midway
puts my hand in ur face in a 'boy bye' like gesture
don't fucking kiss me nigga. i saw u complimenting ole girl on twitta. kiss ha!

people on here are so wild like!!!! u could literally make a post talking about the night u had and it's all specific and shit and like 5 people will reblog it and i'm just like WHY do u need this on ur blog? i don't understand! and then there's the muthafuckas that will reach on a post! like u could make a post saying 'yo i just had an amazing bowl of oatmeal' and some random hoe will come out the cut and say some wild shit like 'wow fuck u not everyone can have oatmeal u assHole' ana I'm just screaming because people on this damn site are so weird and creepy and wild!

push me against the wall and threaten my life because u saw me reblog or like another nigga's tumblr pic. then i'll know it's tru love.

if u wanna be w/ me
delete ur twitta
insta
fb
everything.
worship
me.

i can't wait until everyone understands the concept of not reblogging personal text posts!!!!

tries not to compare myself to all the fine ass girls i see on here every single day

"nigga ain't no body checkin for u!!"
i say
as i close the tab that contains ur twitter page.

if ur white and u reblog posts with the word 'nigga' in it lemme know so i can unfollow yo corny ass.

blocks u for calling me cute instead of sexy

if you don't know what a vulva is, you have no business following me. lmao.

puts on a top that shows a lil cleavage before I FaceTime or Skype a nigga
#LittleHoeThings

him: ur beautiful
me: WHERE THE FUCK WERE U WHEN MY SELFIE DROPPED NIGGA?

complains about my phone being dry

someone calls or texts me
takes forever to reply

biTch u eva been listening to a song so filthy in ur headphones that u turn the volume down a lil bit in fear that others around u might hear?

we're all geeks for still being on this got damn website.

if u facetimin shawty and she put u on pause
she texting another nigga because ur boring to her

yooooooo like i see so many cute black girls on here like every single day that make me wanna do better.

a nigga u rly feelin calls u on skype or facetimes u:
shit lemme put on this cute blouse. lemme put on a lil lipstick. curl my hair. wax my eyebrows *answers*
a nigga u don't give a fuck about calls u on skype or facetimes u:
answers bc no matter how u looking rn u know this nigga gone thirst anyway

oh btw, my blog is a place where black girls are celebrated.
a safe place for black girls.

bitch i'm out here stanning for my own fucking blog.

if i see any low self esteem type posts from ya'll on my dash in 2014 ima reblog ur selfie and force u to stare at it, say i'm beautiful 50 times, and then ima make u message me telling me ur favorite feature about urself.

i need a nigga that's so fucking hood that he don't have time to be on instagram and twitter chatting it up w/ other bitches because he in the streets gettin that money.

i would do a transformation tuesday but i'm not done transforming into my final form yet.

if u white don't be reblogging no post with the word 'nigga' in it! u ain't got no business doing it!
u wanna look like a damn fool? post like a million pics of a nigga that don't even claim u on ur insta while he has zero pics of u on his! don't play urself like that.

what she says: i'm fine
what she really means: u liking otha hoe's pics huh? we playin that game now??!!! since u like her damn pic so much BE WIT HA!!!!!!!!

rolls ova in the bed and taps on ur shoulder at 3 am
why u liking otha hoe's pics on insta?

when i see a fine ass nigga on the dash and then i go to his blog and see nothing but white bitches, his stock goes down immediately idc.

white woman gets ridiculed on social media
a thousand niggas jump out of the bushes to save the damsel in distress
everyone ridicules black women on social media everyday
crickets

JUST TO LET YOU KNOW

THE MOST IMPORTANT LESSON MY PARENTS TAUGHT ME IS IF
YOU'RE BROKE AS FUCK STAY YOUR ASS HOME.

*

a woman is not obligated to show u what she looks like without makeup or weave.

A WOMAN IS NOT OBLIGATED TO SHOW U WHAT SHE LOOKS LIKE WITHOUT MAKEUP OR WEAVE.

white people: everything is not about race! Not all white people are racist geeze u niggers need 2 relax lol

i would rather get no dick than mediocre dick.

no one really fucks w/ me like that irl and i used to think it was because i was a lame and then i realized i am too next level for these hoes.

I'm the type of bitch that goes to extreme lengths to hide food just so I don't have to share it lmao.

no matter how well u 'behave' as a black person, ur life still doesn't matter to white people.

being a black woman isn't rly for the weak hearted. everyday we get some disrespectful outrageous shit thrown at us just for being who we are. imagine waking up everyday and getting dissed and bashed by black men, yt men, shit, every fucking body. for ur hair, ur skin tone, ur weight, every fucking thing.

have some self esteem
some self confidence

stan for urself bitch.

u gotta let the lil brown and black babies know that they matter and that they are crucial! u feel me?

Don't be neutral about ferguson. Either u with us or against us.

in my lil mom voice yo pussy ain't supposed to smell like flowers or candy! don't let these lil fuck niggas or song lyrics fool u into believing that bullshit either. pussy does have a smell. oh and btw yeast infections are totally normal and they are nothing to be ashamed of baby girl. it's just yo vaginal pH balance acting a damn fool. ur not 'gross' or 'nasty' for having one. just pop a diflucan in ma and if that don't work hit yo doctor up. oh and don't let those vagisal commercials make u feel ashamed or embarrassed! pussy is supposed to have an odor! pussy is also self cleansing! pussy grows hair too! these lil boys will try to make u feel bad for having hair on ur pussy because having a 'bald pussy' is considered to be betta for some odd reason. oh and for all my women of color, some parts of ur pussy is going to be darker than others and there is nothing wrong with that! it's still beautiful! pussy comes in all types of shapes and sizes! don't be afraid to look in the mirror at urs! i know it may feel weird or corny but just do it! appreciate ur pussy for the beauty that it is!

we all want attention at some point and time
and there is nothing wrong w/ that
don't let nobody make u feel bad
for wanting attention.

um don't u dare say racism is over.

if we arguin and u ask me if i'm on my period
we throwin hands
what the fuck me being on my menstrual cycle got to do
with u acting like a fuck ass nigga?

moans just to hear myself moan

thinking of all the cute shit i'm gonna buy when i get paid is my favorite thing to think about while i'm at work.

i knew i was grown the day i memorized my social security number bruh.

u hoes be gettin diet soda and gatorade straight playin ya self! the fuck wrong wityall?! give ur body what it truly needs and bust open that water bottle and stop playin games! i can't believe u hoes be sipping on straight sugar then wonder why ur pissing sour ass urine! i'll neva shame a bitch for being a hoe or whateva but ima shame a bitch for drinking soda!

the government makes bullshit foods cheaper than healthier shit so ya'll asses can get sick and buy more medicine and pay for more doctor visits and ultimately die.

I rly don't see why ppl judge strippers, prostitutes, sex workers etc....like who are you to judge someone based on their occupation? stawp worrying about what the fuck that person is doing with their life and worry about what you are doing with YOURS bitch.

ferguson is about racism and the fact that black people live in a system where we're doomed to fail from the womb. this is not about 'poc'. yes other races go thru shit too but black people are at the bottom of the totem pole. this is not a competition of 'which race has it the worst'. black people literally do have it the worst and i'm not just saying that. it's a proven fact. so when u see a post about black people or anything regarding ferguson please don't jump in and say 'well other people of color experience racism' because ferguson is not about other poc. it's about BLACK PEOPLE. B L A C K P E O P L E. don't u dare try to fucking minimize this shit.

from like 9 pm til like 3 a.m. i am....
plottin on my come up
crying about school
crying over the fact that i'm not rich yet
in my feelings

reflecting on the day and what i could have done better
contemplating on life and death
thinking about the shit i need to do tomorrow
on the computer trying to avoid my feelings

shames u for eating white bread

shames u for that can of soda u had yesterday

shames u for not having a favorite fruit

i don't even know if i wanna have kids anymore. i don't want to explain to them that they have to be careful in this world because they are black?

i rarely tell people my problems because when i do tell people them, they never react how i want them to react. people are always casual and non chalant and hit me with that 'it'll be okay' shit and i don't want to hear that!!!!!!!!!

"you just want attention"
me: yeah duh bitch

I tasted myself for the first time today and i'm upset. I taste like a watery soup with no flavor....*sprinkles some seasoning on my clitoris* All those female rappers that tell you their pussy taste like candy and bubblegum are apart of fraudulent advertising. Pussy taste like pussy.

college schoolwork: don't let grades and ur GPA define ur self worth!!!!!
career: don't compare urself to others who may be ahead of u at the moment. ur time will come to shine <3

if a bitch wanna wear makeup to the gym or the pool or whatever....that's her business and it shouldn't be none of ur concern.

You can be fine as fuck & still get cheated on. There's always a bitch with better weave, better pussy, and a better face than yours.

in my lil mom voice baby girl i hope u not washing ur vagina with soaps and shower gels because it's already self cleansing! i don't wanna see ya fuck up ya ph balance tryna make it smell like candy!

u kno u a hoe when yo phone be dry as shit during the day but niggas be blowing yo shit up during booty call hours.

i'm talking to my friend and she's telling me she doesn't like touching herself or looking at her pussy…how you gone let a nigga touch you when you don't even touch yo self?

no matter how insecure i'm feeling about my appearance or whatever, i would never down the next bitch who's doing her thing. like i'm not going to hate or project my insecurities on to her. That's childish and petty. bitches who hate on fly pretty girls are the worst. they are ugly on the inside as well as the outside.

if u not helping me grow, u gosta go.

u can truly do it all!!!! u can be a hoe, a queen, a thot, a bad bitch, a princess,
U CAN BE
ALLAAAAAAHHHHDATTT SIMULTANEOUSLY MA!

the best skin care product on the market is h20. waTUR. agua.

when i was a little girl, everytime i played with my barbies it was like a jerry springer episode bruh. broken homes, marriage, divorce, infidelity, domestic violence. I would talk all the voices including the male parts and would just entertain myself for hours and hours. mannnnn.

i'm grown but i'm still uh lil childish frm time 2 time.

did u
drink enough
water today?

swerves out of my lane to get a bitch together real quick

gets back in my lane

tell every little black girl u see that she's beautiful and important and special and worthy of being loved.

Shit I love about being on my period:
1. It gives me a valid excuse to act like a complete cunt.
2. My mother and my friends display sympathy for me when I tell them i'm on it.
3. When niggars hit me up asking for dirty pictures, I can send them a picture of a bloody pad if I want to.
4. I can be a total bitch and blame it on my hormones. (refer to number one)
5. I can lay in bed all day, cry, and bitch about shit that no one gives a fuck about.

brown skin looks amazing with every color.

ima crazy ass bitch. i really am. i will fina receipts. i will look thru every tweet, every insta pic. ima detective ass bitch. don't think u can lie to me and i won't find out. i'm omnipresent. I FIND OUT EVERYTHING MY NIGGA. EVERYTHING. some shit u done did a year ago, i know about. i'm hip to the got damn game.

spends 80% of my money on food

public service announcement: just because ole girl got in a 22 inch malaysian sew in doesn't mean she loves herself any less than baby girl with the afro puffs.

u wanna change ur mood? stop eating processed foods. all the damn ingredients u can't even pronounce are making u tired and sad.

stop making other women feel bad for wearing makeup.

stop making other women feel bad for wearing weave.

stop making other women feel bad for the way they want to carry themselves or dress.

just because u don't wear makeup or wear a weave doesn't make u any better than the next woman.

stop saying shit like 'i'm a natural beauty'.

if any woman wanna wear makeup, weave, etc. to feel beautiful, let her do that.

LET HER LIVE. SHE AIN'T HURTING NOBODY.

WE ALL DO CERTAIN SHIT TO FEEL GOOD ABOUT OUR APPEARANCE.

sometimes u just gotta admit 2 ya self that ur a geek ass bitch and accept it and be okay wit it.

why do i run into ppl on the days i look hit but when i look cute, no one is around to see!!!! what the fuck!

a poem by me:

sorry i can't come out to play

i'm having a bad skin and hair day

in order to be a bad bitch u gotta leave that soda alone ma.

don't sleep on quiet low-key girls! we are the nastiest. we the typa bitches that keep suckin after u nutted! don't sleep on us!

i literally want to stab anyone that's ever told me 'u sound so white'.

survival tips

stay hydrated

stay cute

stay lowkey

stay in ur lane

That awkward moment when you're out in public and your pubes start to itch and You attempt to discretely scratch them. Don't fucking tell me that shit hasn't happened to you bitch.

first date questions: What do u think about Beyoncé? Do U Eat Ass?

1.if u see a bad bitch doing her thing, give her props 2. never let these fuck niggas make u feel any type of way about urself 3. never put any dick before ur girl or girl crew 4. never be pressed over a nigga. especially a nigga that isn't urs. 5. close ur legs to married men 6. know ur the shit, no nigga's approval needed.

um just a friendly reminder that i don't share dick or food!!!!!

my pussy will make ya wanna go back 2 school and get cha masters

imagine saying yahh trick yahh to ur moms when she asked u to do the dishes.

u know u starting to catch feelings when u like the way their name looks on ur phone when they text u. please stay woke.

i never judge ppl who commit suicide. you don't know what that person is going thru mentally and emotionally to get to such a place where they want to take their own life.

if showing empathy for others makes me a corny ass hoe then so be it, i'm a corny ass hoe!!!!!

i used to be really judgmental towards people who have gotten plastic surgery but now i realize that there is absolutely nothing wrong with doing something that will make u feel better about urself. we all want to look in the mirror and feel like we look our absolute best. Plastic surgery doesn't have to always stem from 'self hate'. it can really just be that person wanting to improve themselves and be a better version of themselves.

clears throat don't let anyone tell u that being 'selfish' is bad. like? loving the fuck out of urself and doing what's best for u and what benefits u is a great thing as long as u ain't hurting nobody or lying about ur intentions like?

ij baby girl ain't got no edges, don't drag ha!!! put shawty on!!!! give her some links to some youtube vids! give her some of ur castor oil! help baby girl get back on her feet instead of knocking her while she down!!!!!!!

be aware of what's going on with ur body
if u gotta weird cough or discharge leaking from places it ain't supposed to
go to the doctor rn

love urself

google will have u paranoid and thinking u dying of AIDS or some shit

going to the doctor can cause anxiousness but i rather know what's up than not know

u feel me?

being a hoe is lots of fun. don't let no one convince u otha wise.

when i was younger i used to have so much anxiety about being an adult and having responsibilities. i used to think to myself 'how does my mom know which brand of detergent to buy?'

everybody cuffed but me:

a memoir

u know u a hoe when u can't remember which nude u've sent to a nigga already and ur genuinely confused on which nigga got which nudes.

'u have so much to be grateful for!' is one of those things u shouldn't tell someone who is depressed. sometimes, a person is not depressed about a situation that is going on in their lives. sometimes a person is just depressed because of the way they feel about themselves. sometimes that person just wants to be heard. They want someone to listen to them. They don't want someone that is going to dismiss their feelings and make them feel like they are overreacting or 'letting things get them down'. Negative thoughts can cloud a person's mind so much that they cannot even get out of bed to do small simple tasks like brush their teeth or change out of their pajamas. I hate it when people who commit suicide are judged and deemed 'selfish'. Or people will say 'wow didn't they think of their family?'. U are not in that person's shoes. U don't know their mental space. U don't know how much energy it takes for them to go about their day. U don't know how negative situations can cloud their judgment or make them feel worthless about themselves.

every day i thank God that i don't look

like i did

in 2009, 2010, 2011, or 2012.

things i think about while i'm at work
money
dick

a white girl when she finds out she's been cheated on: *wow omg! i can't believe u would do this to me!*

a black girl when she finds out she's been cheated on: *OHHH SO U FUCKIN OTHA HOES NOW HUH??!???!!!?????!!!!???!*

once i take my bra off, don't ask me to do shit for u bitch bc once that bra comes off, i am clocked out of life. i am done. i am finished. i am logged the fuck out.

if u compare me to another bitch, be prepared to square up because i'm the best thing that's eva happened to u.

look if we go together
u better act like ur fucking blind
i better be the only bitch u attracted to

break off any one sided friendships. don't let these hoes talk ur ear off about their ain't shit niggas but then they don't bother to ask about u! u deserve betta 2k14.

calls myself out for being a fake bitch before u even have the chance to do it

if u not fucking with me 100% and supporting me and helping me grow into a better person then get the fuck away from me! no one is getting in the way of my personal progress!!!!!!

don't let nobody shame u for what kind of job u do. whether it's cleaning a toilet or being a sex worker, don't let these broke bitches make u feel any type of way about how u get ur money. money is money.

if I farted in your face, would you still love me?

"u wanna chill today?"
me: nah
"why?"
me: i'm having a bad hair day sorry

if we go together, u better speak about me like that crazy ass nigga did on the beginning of 'love sosa' or our relationship will never work.

i need friends that will keep it all the way real
like "u gotta huge ass booger hanging out of ur nose ma" or will have the heart to tell me if my weave is looking hit.
like not in a malicious way but in a girl, i care for u and i want u to look good kind of way.

when someone tries to shame u for being a hoe they only tryna stop u from living ur life and having fun.

if u ever think about being dishonest w/ me don't try it bc i always find shit out. i'm a detective and i always keep note of what you've said no matter how long ago it was. when i accuse u of some shit, i will never come at u without receipts of ur dishonesty

u know what takes some real balls?
ordering jeans off the inanet!

me: i can't cook!
my family and friends: girl u ain't neva gone get married
me: ima wife up myself

if a bitch wanna show some titties and ass! let ha live!!!! LET HA!!!!! all u niggas that are screaming 'she's a hoe' 'no one would eva wife her' 'she out there' are the same niggas that are beating ur meat to ha pics at night and nutting in ur socks wishing u had a bitch like her look ur way!

hobbies: looking at expensive ass clothes and shoes on the internet that i can't afford

fake recognize fake and u lookin real familiar 2 me.

president and CEO of team clear pee

if she got a michael kors or coach bag she fuck raw.

me on the phone: TRUUUUUUUU!!!!!!! TRUUUUUUUUUUUUUUUUUU!!!!!!!!!!!!!!!!! TRRRRRUUUUUUUUUUU!

busts it open
sees that ur not giving me all of ur attention
closes it back up

for those who asked me what i've been eating…..
for breakfast, i typically eat either oatmeal or…. 2 boiled eggs and 2 pieces of whole wheat bread!
for snacks, i eat fruit and almonds!
for lunch, i eat shit like brown rice, green beans, and turkey!
for dinner, i'll eat red beans with brown rice!
i cut out fast food completely! i drink water with all of my meals and in-between meals as well! i carry my water bottles with me everywhere as a visual reminder for me to drink more water! i don't eat white bread, white rice, or any white flour! if it's white, it ain't right loool. the only meat i eat is turkey! i don't eat any cookies, cakes, or pastries! if i'm craving something sweet, a few spoonfuls of peanut butter will satisfy my sweet tooth! i also have a cute lil lunch bag that i keep my snacks in so i won't be caught out and about and tempted to eat bullshit! i pack shit in my lunch bag the night before! it's all about being prepared! :)

everytime i take a shit, i thank God because that lets me know that thangs are running smoothly in my body and i'm getting rid of waste and toxins man. like God my homie for allowing me to do that every other day.

it's crazy how u can miss someone even if they treated u like shit????

911: what's ur emergency?
me: THESE HOES *gasps for air* WON'T *breathes heavily* LET ME LIVE

i talk to myself every single day and bitch me and myself be having some fiyah ass conversations! wooooo!

da facts of life: no matter how fine u are, u could still get cheated on.

if a bitch don't get jealous or feel some typa way when u chat it up with otha hoes, she don't love u!!!!!!

don't let a hoe that eats white bread and drinks soda tell u shit about urself.

thirsting on or liking other ppl's seflies while u in a relationship is disrespectful as hell to ur partner because ur partner may compare themselves to that person's pic u just liked. don't put ur bae thru that.

#teamCantTakeDick

my favorite hobby is rolling my eyes.

there's so much pressure in the spring to plan out ur hoe looks for the summa.

ima good friend because u can tell me anything and i won't make u feel embarrassed or ashamed! u could say some shit like 'girl i been having this weird discharge for like the past week' and i'll be like 'wow babe are u okay?' instead of 'DAMN BITCH EWWW WTF'.

when i'm say 'i'm feelin some typa way' it could mean two different thangs. it could either mean i'm not in a good mood or I'm horny as hell.

1. that boy got me feelin some typa way = i wanna do a coupla thangs

2. i'm feelin some typa way today and i don't want to talk rn = i'm not in a good mood. it's best to leave me alone.

knocks on ur front door

DID U DRINK ENOUGH WATER TODAY?
DID U GET ENOUGH FIBER BAE??

i love hanging out with myself but i get lonely as hell and i want a real ass friend that won't judge me or won't lie to me or make me feel shitty about myself or just someone that genuinely will listen to the dumb ass shit i get upset about and don't just wait for their turn to talk and let me be the one to talk for once.

when i compliment someone, i mean it so much!!! because i'm very quiet and not talkative at all unless i know u know u! so if i go out of my way to compliment u, i genuinely mean it!!!!!

ij baby girl wanna be a hoe who are u to tell her she can't! LET HER LIVE HER LIFE. don't police her sexuality u emma nelson ass bitch.

i had an epiphany that u raggedy hoes will never let me live my life but ima still do it regardless.

i'm apart of #teamChill and #teamDoingTheMost at the same time.

i talk to myself a lot because i got good conversation and ion trust u hoes.

i don't like sex but i like it at the same time. i'm real and fake. i don't want to be bothered but i love attention. i complain about how annoying niggas are yet i still talk to them. i'm a walking contradiction.

a poem by me:

when
will the sun
come back
i'm
ready
2
be
a hoe.

falls back forever

it makes people uncomfortable when someone is feeling themselves hard. low-key, some people love to see others with low self esteem or low self confidence because that's how they feel about themselves. they neea somethin to relate to.

do whatever u need to do to feel good about urself and ur physical appearance and don't let nobody shame u for it! whether that be getting plastic surgery or trying a new hairstyle!!! it's ur body! it's ur face! it's ur hair! and it's nobody business! if that purple lipstick makes u feel like a bad bitch, wear it! if u wanna get a 22 inch sew in or rock a fresh ass fade, by all means do that ma! if u wanna get ur breasts done or ur ass done, that's cool too!

Final Words

Hey babies!!!!!! i just want to say thank u to everyone that fucks with me and my blog. thank u for all of the sweet and sincere messages and fanmail i have received. Thank u for allowing me to express my thoughts and opinions and just allowing a bitch to be herself!!!!!! God knows i'm not perfect but ya'll love me and accept me for the person that i am anyway. U guys provide encouragement and u believe in me and that's fucking incredible!!!! stay positive. stay cute. Mind ya business. stay in ur lane. don't let these fuck niggas make u doubt ya self and make sure ur drinkin enough water. i love ya'll!!!!!!

-Chelsea a.k.a. Pinkvelourtracksuit

Made in the USA
Charleston, SC
29 June 2015